Windows® 95

VISUAL POCKETGUIDE

IDG's **3-D Visual** Series

IDG
BOOKS
From
maranGraphics™

IDG Books Worldwide, Inc.
An International Data Group Company
Foster City, CA • Indianapolis • Chicago • Dallas

Windows® 95 Visual PocketGuide

Published by
IDG Books Worldwide, Inc.
An International Data Group Company
919 E. Hillsdale Blvd., Suite 400
Foster City, CA 94404
(415) 655-3000

Copyright© 1995 by maranGraphics Inc.
5755 Coopers Avenue
Mississauga, Ontario, Canada
L4Z 1R9

Screen shots reprinted with permission from Microsoft Corporation.

Library of Congress Catalog Card No.: 95-076878
ISBN: 1-56884-661-4
Printed in the United States of America
10 9 8 7 6

Distributed in the United States by IDG Books Worldwide, Inc.

Distributed by Computer and Technical Books in Miami, Florida, for South America and the Caribbean; by Longman Singapore in Singapore, Malaysia, Thailand, and Korea; by Toppan Co. Ltd. in Japan; by IDG Communications HK in Hong Kong; by WoodsLane Pty. Ltd. in Australia and New Zealand; and by Transworld Publishers Ltd. in the U.K. and Europe.

For general information on IDG Books in the U.S., including information on discounts and premiums, contact IDG Books at 800-762-2974 or 317-895-5200.

For U.S. Corporate Sales and quantity discounts, contact maranGraphics at 800-469-6616, ext. 206.

For information on international sales of IDG Books, contact Helen Saraceni at 415-655-3021, Fax number 415-655-3295.

For information on translations, contact Marc Jeffrey Mikulich, Director of Rights and Licensing, at IDG Books Worldwide. Fax Number 415-655-3295.

For sales inquiries and special prices for bulk quantities, write to the address above or call IDG Books Worldwide at 415-655-3000.

For information on using IDG Books in the classroom, or ordering examination copies, contact Jim Kelly at 800-434-2086.

Trademark Acknowledgments

©1995
maranGraphics, Inc.

The animated characters are the
copyright of maranGraphics, Inc.

U.S. Corporate Sales	U.S. Trade Sales
Contact maranGraphics at (800) 469-6616, ext. 206 or Fax (905) 890-9434.	Contact IDG Books at (800) 434-3422 or (415) 655-3000.

About IDG Books Worldwide

Welcome to the world of IDG Books Worldwide.

IDG Books Worldwide, Inc., is a subsidiary of International Data Group, the world's largest publisher of business and computer-related information and the leading global provider of information services on information technology. IDG was founded more than 25 years ago and now employs more than 5,700 people worldwide. IDG publishes more than 200 computer publications in 63 countries (see listing below). Forty million people read one or more IDG publications each month.

Launched in 1990, IDG Books is today the fastest-growing publisher of computer and business books in the United States. We are proud to have received 3 awards from the Computer Press Association in recognition of editorial excellence, and our best-selling ...For Dummies series has more than 10 million copies in print with translations in more than 20 languages. IDG Books, through a recent joint venture with IDG's Hi-Tech Beijing, became the first U.S. publisher to publish a computer book in the People's Republic of China. In record time, IDG Books has become the first choice for millions of readers around the world who want to learn how to better manage their businesses.

Our mission is simple: Every IDG book is designed to bring extra value and skill-building instructions to the reader. Our books are written by experts who understand and care about our readers. The knowledge base of our editorial staff comes from years of experience in publishing, education, and journalism — experience which we use to produce books for the '90s. In short, we care about books, so we attract the best people. We devote special attention to details such as audience, interior design, use of icons, and illustrations. And because we use an efficient process of authoring, editing, and desktop publishing our books electronically, we can spend more time ensuring superior content and spend less time on the technicalities of making books.

You can count on our commitment to deliver high-quality books at competitive prices on topics customers want to read about. At IDG, we value quality, and we have been delivering quality for more than 25 years. You'll find no better book on a subject than an IDG book.

John Kilcullen
President and CEO
IDG Books Worldwide, Inc.

IDG Books Worldwide, Inc., is a subsidiary of International Data Group. The officers are Patrick J. McGovern, Founder and Board Chairman; Walter Boyd, President. International Data Group's publications include: ARGENTINA'S Computerworld Argentina, Infoworld Argentina; AUSTRALIA'S Computerworld Australia, Australian PC World, Australian Macworld, Network World, Mobile Business Australia, Reseller, IDG Sources; AUSTRIA'S Computerwelt Oesterreich, PC Test; BRAZIL'S Computerworld, Gamepro, Game Power, Mundo IBM, Mundo Unix, PC World, Super Game; BELGIUM'S Data News (CW) BULGARIA'S Computerworld Bulgaria, Ediworld, PC & Mac World Bulgaria, Network World Bulgaria; CANADA'S CIO Canada, Computerworld Canada, Graduate Computerworld, InfoCanada, Network World Canada; CHILE'S Computerworld Chile, Informatica; COLOMBIA'S Computerworld Colombia, PC World; CZECH REPUBLIC'S Computerworld, Elektronika, PC World; DENMARK'S Communications World, Computerworld Danmark, Macintosh Produktkatalog, Macworld Danmark, PC World Danmark, PC World Produktguide, Tech World, Windows World; ECUADOR'S PC World Ecuador; EGYPT'S Computerworld (CW) Middle East, PC World Middle East; FINLAND'S MikroPC, Tietoviikko, Tietoverkko; FRANCE'S Distributique, GOLDEN MAC, InfoPC, Languages & Systems, Le Guide du Monde Informatique, Le Monde Informatique, Telecoms & Reseaux; GERMANY'S Computerwoche, Computerwoche Focus, Computerwoche Extra, Computerwoche Karriere, Information Management, Macwelt, Netzwelt, PC Welt, PC Woche, Publish, Unit; GREECE'S Infoworld, PC Games; HUNGARY'S Computerworld SZT, PC World; HONG KONG'S Computerworld Hong Kong, PC World Hong Kong, INDIA'S Computers & Communications; IRELAND'S ComputerScope; ISRAEL'S Computerworld Israel, PC World Israel; ITALY'S Computerworld Italia, Lotus Magazine, Macworld Italia, Networking Italia, PC Shopping, PC World Italia; JAPAN'S Computerworld Today, Information Systems World, Macworld Japan, Nikkei Personal Computing, SunWorld Japan, Windows World; KENYA'S East African Computer News; KOREA'S Computerworld Korea, Macworld Korea, PC World Korea; MEXICO'S Compu Edicion, Compu Manufactura, Computacion/Punto de Venta, Computerworld Mexico, MacWorld, Mundo Unix, PC World, Windows; THE NETHERLANDS' Computer! Totaal, Computable (CW), LAN Magazine, MacWorld, Totaal "Windows"; NEW ZEALAND'S Computer Listings, Computerworld New Zealand, New Zealand PC World, Network World; NIGERIA'S PC World Africa; NORWAY'S Computerworld Norge, C/World, Lotusworld Norge, Macworld Norge, Networld, PC World Ekspress, PC World Norge, PC World's Produktguide, Publish& Multimedia World, Student Data, Unix World, Windowsworld; IDG Direct Response; PAKISTAN'S PC World Pakistan; PANAMA'S PC World Panama; PERU'S Computerworld Peru, PC World; PEOPLE'S REPUBLIC OF CHINA'S China Computerworld, China Infoworld, Electronics Today/Multimedia World, Electronics International, Electronic Product World, China Network World, PC and Communications Magazine, PC World China, Software World Magazine, Telecom Product World; IDG HIGH TECH BEIJING'S New Product World; IDG SHENZHEN'S Computer News Digest; PHILIPPINES' Computerworld Philippines, PC Digest (PCW); POLAND'S Computerworld Poland, PC World/Komputer; PORTUGAL'S Cerebro/PC World, Correio Informatico/Computerworld, Informatica & Comunicacoes Catalogo, MacIn, Nacional de Produtos; ROMANIA'S Computerworld, PC World; RUSSIA'S Computerworld-Moscow, Mir - PC, Sety; SINGAPORE'S Computerworld Southeast Asia, PC World Singapore; SLOVENIA'S Monitor Magazine; SOUTH AFRICA'S Computer Mail (CIO),Computing S.A ,Network World S.A., Software World; SPAIN'S Advanced Systems, Amiga World, Computerworld Espana, Communicaciones World, Macworld Espana, NeXTWORLD, Super Juegos Magazine (GamePro), PC World Espana, Publish, SWEDEN'S Attack, ComputerSweden, Corporate Computing, Natverk & Kommunikation, Macworld, Mikrodatorn, PC World, Publishing & Design (CAP), Datalngenjoren, Maxi Data,Windows World; SWITZERLAND'S Computerworld Schweiz, Macworld Schweiz, PC Tip; TAIWAN'S Computerworld Taiwan, PC World Taiwan; THAILAND'S Thai Computerworld; TURKEY'S Computerworld Monitor, Macworld Turkiye, PC World Turkiye; UKRAINE'S Computerworld; UNITED KINGDOM'S Computing /Computerworld, Connexion/Network World, Lotus Magazine, Macworld, Open Computing/Sunworld; UNITED STATES' Advanced Systems, AmigaWorld, Cable in the Classroom, CD Review, CIO, Computerworld, Digital Video, DOS Resource Guide, Electronic Entertainment Magazine, Federal Computer Week, Federal Integrator, GamePro, IDG Books, Infoworld, Infoworld Direct, Laser Event, Macworld, Multimedia World, Network World, PC Letter, PC World, PlayRight, Power PC World, Publish, SWATPro, Video Event; VENEZUELA'S Computerworld Venezuela, PC World; VIETNAM'S PC World Vietnam

Every maranGraphics book represents the extraordinary vision and commitment of a unique family: the Maran family of Toronto, Canada.

Back Row (from left to right):
Sherry Maran, Rob Maran, mG, Richard Maran, Maxine Maran, Jill Maran.
Front Row (from left to right): *mG, Judy Maran, Ruth Maran, mG.*

Richard Maran is the company founder and its inspirational leader. He began maranGraphics over twenty years ago with a vision of a more efficient way to communicate a visual grammar that fuses text and graphics and allows readers to instantly grasp concepts.

Ruth Maran is the Author and Architect—a role Richard established that now bears Ruth's distinctive touch. She creates the words and visual structure that are the basis for the books.

Judy Maran is Senior Editor. She works with Ruth, Richard, and the highly talented maranGraphics illustrators, designers, and editors to transform Ruth's material into its final form.

Rob Maran is the Technical and Production Specialist. He makes sure the state-of-the-art technology used to create these books always performs as it should.

Sherry Maran manages the Reception, Order Desk, and any number of areas that require immediate attention and a helping hand.

Jill Maran is a jack-of-all-trades and dynamo who fills in anywhere she's needed any time she's back from university.

Maxine Maran is the Business Manager and family sage. She maintains order in the business and family—and keeps everything running smoothly.

Oh, and there's **mG**. He's maranGraphics' spokesperson and, well, star. When you use a maranGraphics book, you'll see a lot of mG and his friends. They're just part of the family!

Acknowledgments

Thanks to the dedicated staff of maranGraphics, including David de Haas, Francisco Ferreira, Brad Hilderley, Chris K.C. Leung, Paul Lofthouse, Jill Maran, Judy Maran, Maxine Maran, Robert Maran, Sherry Maran, Russ Marini, Neil Mohan, Tamara Poliquin, Dave Ross, Andrew Trowbridge, Christie Van Duin, and Kelleigh Wing.

Thanks also to Saverio C. Tropiano for his assistance and expert advice.

Finally, to Richard Maran who originated the easy-to-use graphic format of this guide. Thank you for your inspiration and guidance.

Credits

Author & Architect: Ruth Maran	*Layout Designers:* David de Haas Christie Van Duin	*Editors:* Brad Hilderley Paul Lofthouse Judy Maran
Technical Consultant: Wendi Blouin Ewbank	*Illustrators:* Dave Ross Tamara Poliquin	*Post Production:* Robert Maran
Copy Developer & Editor: Kelleigh Wing	*Screen Artist:* Andrew Trowbridge	

TABLE OF CONTENTS

GETTING STARTED

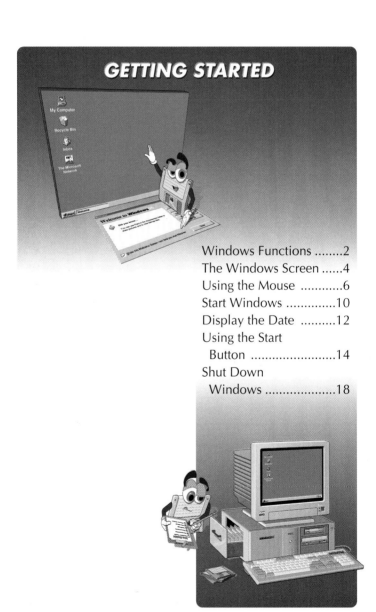

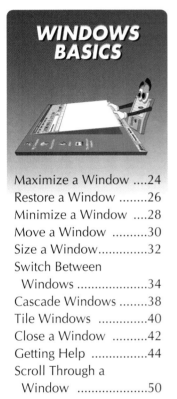

WINDOWS BASICS

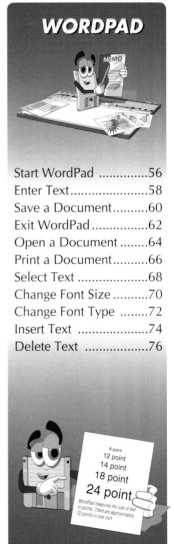

WORDPAD

8 point
12 point
14 point
18 point
24 point

WordPad measures the size of text
in points. There are approximately
72 points in one inch.

TABLE OF CONTENTS

PAINT

VIEW CONTENTS OF COMPUTER

WORK WITH FILES

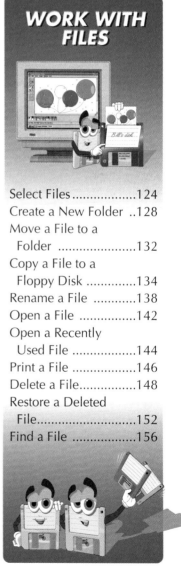

TABLE OF CONTENTS

CHANGE WINDOWS SETTINGS

MAINTAIN YOUR COMPUTER

GETTING STARTED

WINDOWS FUNCTIONS

Microsoft® Windows® 95 is a program that controls the overall activity of your computer.

Like an orchestra conductor, Windows ensures that all parts of your computer work together smoothly and efficiently.

CONTROLS YOUR HARDWARE

Windows controls the different parts of your computer system, such as the printer and monitor, and enables them to work together.

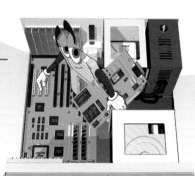

RUNS YOUR PROGRAMS

Windows starts and operates programs, such as Microsoft Word and Lotus 1-2-3. Programs let you write letters, analyze numbers, manage finances, draw pictures and even play games.

Note: Windows comes with several useful programs. These include a word processor (WordPad) and a drawing program (Paint).

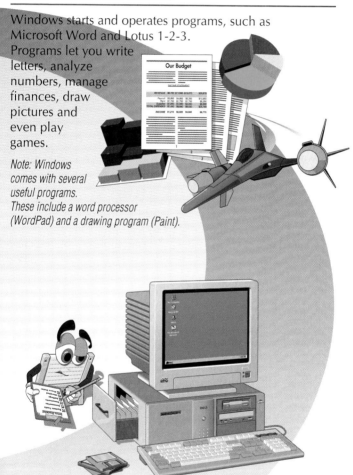

ORGANIZES YOUR INFORMATION

Windows provides ways to organize and manage files stored on your computer. You can use Windows to sort, copy, move, delete and view your files.

THE WINDOWS SCREEN

RECYCLE BIN

Stores all the files you delete and allows you to recover them later.

START BUTTON

Gives you quick access to programs and files.

The Windows screen displays various items. The items that appear depend on how your computer is set up.

MY COMPUTER

Lets you view all the folders and files stored on your computer.

TITLE BAR

Displays the name of an open window.

WINDOW

A rectangle on your screen that displays information.

TASKBAR

Displays the name of each open window on your screen. This lets you easily switch between the open windows.

USING THE MOUSE

◆ Hold the mouse as shown in the diagram. Use your thumb and two rightmost fingers to move the mouse while your two remaining fingers press the mouse buttons.

6

The mouse is a hand-held device that lets you select and move items on your screen.

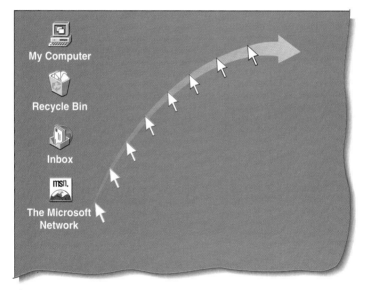

My Computer

Recycle Bin

Inbox

msn.

The Microsoft Network

◆ When you move the mouse on your desk, the mouse pointer ⟨ on your screen moves in the same direction. The mouse pointer assumes different shapes (examples: ⟨, I), depending on its location on your screen and the task you are performing.

USING THE MOUSE

PARTS OF THE MOUSE

◆ The mouse has a left and right button. You can use these buttons to select commands and choose options.

MOUSE TERMS

CLICK

Press and release the left mouse button.

DOUBLE-CLICK

Quickly press and release the left mouse button twice.

◆ A ball under the mouse senses movement. To ensure smooth motion of the mouse, you should occasionally remove and clean this ball.

DRAG AND DROP

When the mouse pointer is over an object on your screen, press and hold down the left mouse button. Still holding down the button, move the mouse to where you want to place the object and then release the button.

START WINDOWS

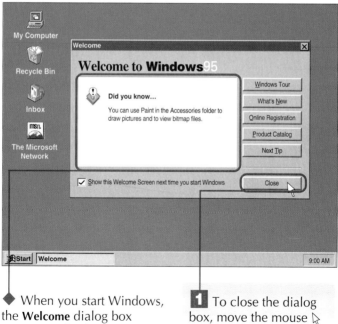

◆ When you start Windows, the **Welcome** dialog box appears. It displays a tip about using Windows.

1 To close the dialog box, move the mouse ⬚ over **Close** and then press the left button.

10

Windows provides an easy, graphical way for you to use your computer.

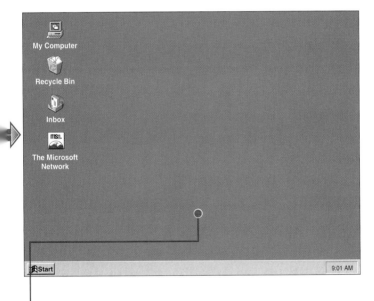

◆ The dialog box disappears and you can clearly view your desktop. The **desktop** is the background area of your screen.

DISPLAY THE DATE

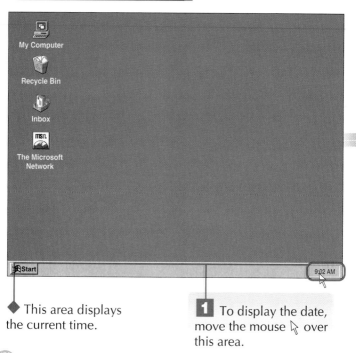

My Computer

Recycle Bin

Inbox

The Microsoft Network

Start   9:02 AM

◆ This area displays the current time.

1 To display the date, move the mouse ⬉ over this area.

You can easily display the date on your screen.

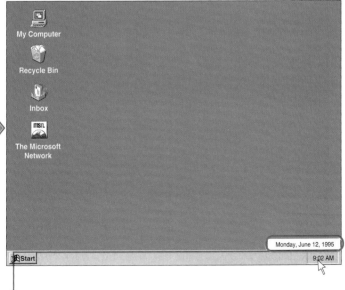

◆ After a few seconds, the date appears.

Note: If Windows displays the wrong date or time, you can change the date or time set in your computer. For more information, refer to page 164.

USING THE START BUTTON

USING THE START BUTTON

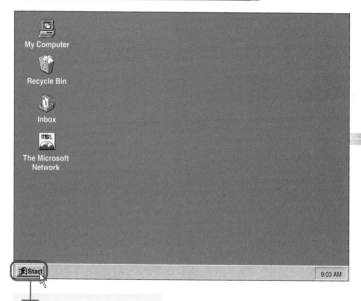

My Computer

Recycle Bin

Inbox

The Microsoft Network

Start   9:03 AM

1 Move the mouse ⌖ over **Start** and then press the left button.

◆ A menu appears.

The Start button lets you display a list of items. You can choose from these items to perform specific tasks in Windows.

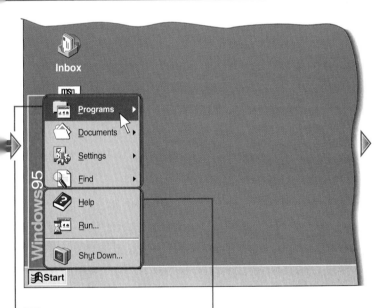

2 To select an item that displays an arrow (▸), move the mouse ⃗ over the item (example: **Programs**). Another menu appears.

◆ To select an item that does not display an arrow, move the mouse ⃗ over the item (example: **Help**) and then press the left button.

CONTINUED

15

USING THE START BUTTON

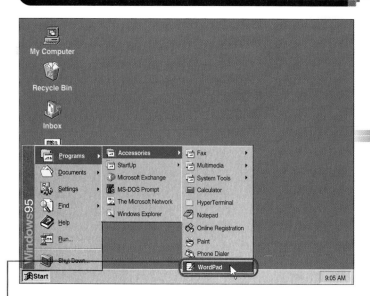

3 Repeat step **2** until you see the item you want to select (example: **WordPad**).

4 Move the mouse ⌖ over the item and then press the left button.

*Note: To close the **Start** menu without selecting an item, move the mouse ⌖ outside the menu area and then press the left button.*

16

Each menu
that appears narrows
your options. This makes
it easier to find the
item you want.

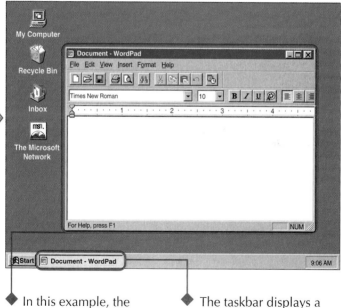

◆ In this example, the
WordPad window appears
on your screen.

*Note: For information on using
WordPad, refer to the WordPad
chapter, starting on page 56.*

◆ The taskbar displays a
button for the open window.

*Note: To close a window to remove it
from your screen, refer to page 42.*

17

SHUT DOWN WINDOWS

SHUT DOWN WINDOWS

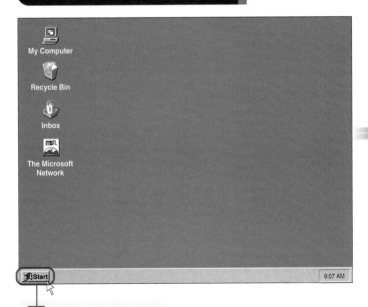

1 Move the mouse ⌖ over **Start** and then press the left button.

When you
finish using Windows,
you can shut down
the program.

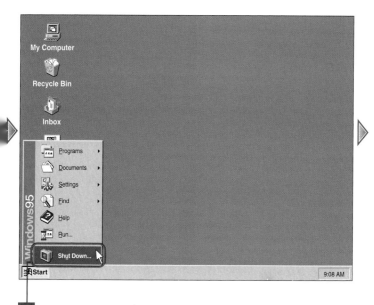

2 Move the mouse ⌖ over
Shut Down and then press the
left button.

CONTINUED

SHUT DOWN WINDOWS

SHUT DOWN WINDOWS (CONTINUED)

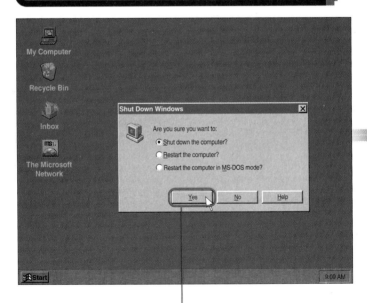

Shut Down Windows

Are you sure you want to:
- Shut down the computer?
- Restart the computer?
- Restart the computer in MS-DOS mode?

Yes   No   Help

◆ The **Shut Down Windows** dialog box appears.

3 To shut down your computer, move the mouse ↘ over **Yes** and then press the left button.

To avoid damaging your information, you must shut down Windows before turning off your computer.

It's now safe to turn off your computer.

◆ You can now safely turn off your computer.

In this chapter you will learn the basic skills you need to work in Windows.

WINDOWS
BASICS

MAXIMIZE A WINDOW

MAXIMIZE A WINDOW

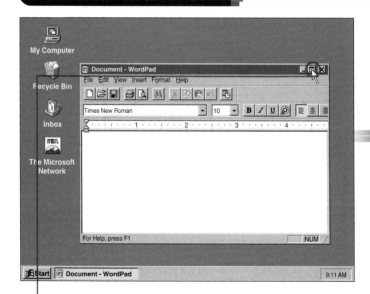

1 Move the mouse ⌖ over 🔲 in the window you want to enlarge and then press the left button.

Note: To display the WordPad window, perform steps **1** *to* **4** *on page 56.*

24

You can enlarge a window to fill your screen. This lets you view more of its contents.

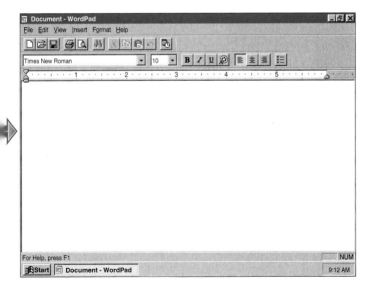

◆ The window fills your screen.

RESTORE A WINDOW

RESTORE A WINDOW

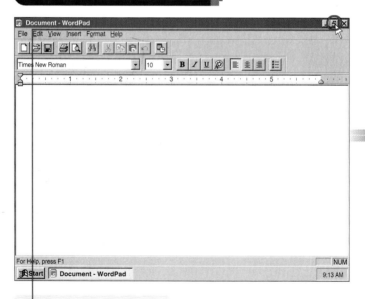

1 Move the mouse ▷ over 🗗 in the window you want to restore and then press the left button.

Note: Only maximized windows display the Restore button (🗗).

26

You can return a maximized window to its previous size. This lets you view information hidden behind the window.

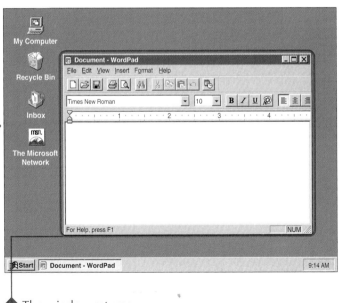

◆ The window returns to its previous size.

MINIMIZE A WINDOW

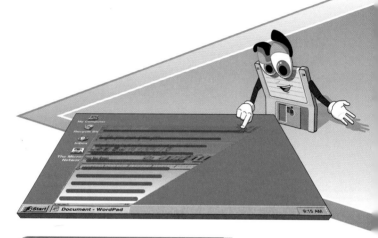

MINIMIZE A WINDOW

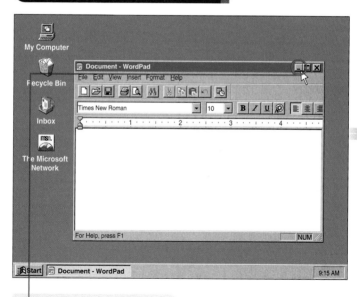

1 Move the mouse ⟨⟩ over ▬ in the window you want to minimize and then press the left button.

28

If you are not using a window, you can minimize the window to remove it from your screen. You can redisplay the window at any time.

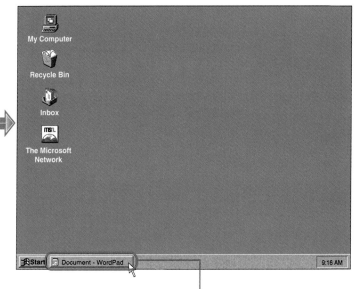

◆ The window disappears.

2 To redisplay the window on your screen, move the mouse ⬚ over its button on the taskbar and then press the left button.

29

MOVE A WINDOW

If a window covers items on your screen, you can move the window to a different location.

MOVE A WINDOW

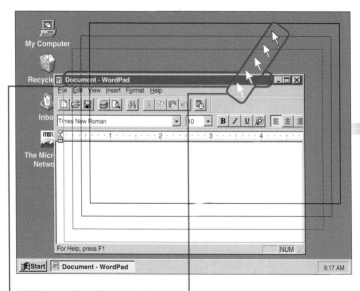

1 Move the mouse ⤏ over the title bar of the window you want to move.

2 Press and hold down the left button as you drag the mouse ⤏ to where you want to place the window.

◆ An outline of the window indicates the new location.

30

3 Release the button and the window moves to the new location.

SIZE A WINDOW

SIZE A WINDOW

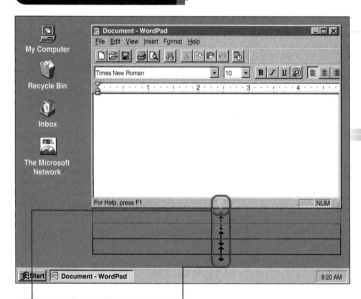

1 Move the mouse ▷ over an edge of the window you want to size and ▷ changes to ↕.

2 Press and hold down the left button.

3 Still holding down the button, drag the mouse ↕ until the outline of the window displays the size you want.

32

You can easily change the size of a window displayed on your screen.

- Enlarging a window lets you view more of its contents.

- Reducing a window lets you view items covered by the window.

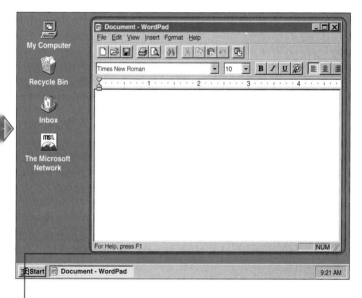

4 Release the button and the window changes to the new size.

Note: You can change the size of a window from any edge or corner.

SWITCH BETWEEN WINDOWS

SWITCH BETWEEN WINDOWS

◆ In this example, the Start button is used to open the **Paint** window.

Note: To use the Start button, refer to page 14.

You can have more than one window open at the same time.

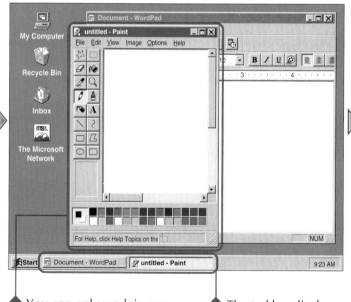

◆ You can only work in one window at a time. The active window (example: **Paint**) appears in front of all other windows.

◆ The taskbar displays a button for each open window on your screen.

CONTINUED

35

SWITCH BETWEEN WINDOWS

SWITCH WINDOWS (CONTINUED)

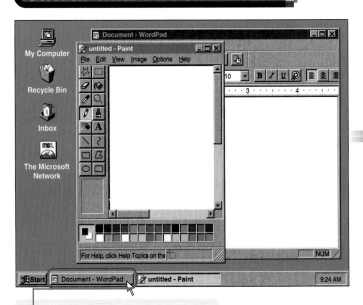

1 To move the window you want to work with to the front, move the mouse ▷ over its button on the taskbar (example: **WordPad**) and then press the left button.

Think of each window as a separate piece of paper. You can rearrange the papers so the one you want to work with is on top.

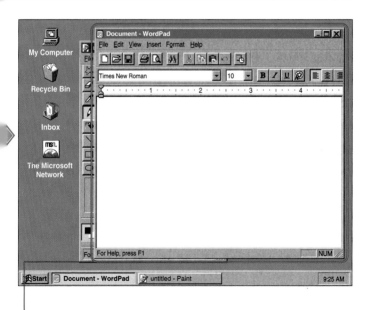

◆ The window appears in front of all other windows.

CASCADE WINDOWS

CASCADE WINDOWS

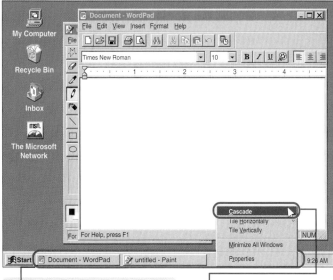

1 Move the mouse ⊳ over an empty area on the taskbar and then press the **right** button. A menu appears.

2 Move the mouse ⊳ over **Cascade** and then press the left button.

38

If you have several windows open, some of them may be hidden from view. The Cascade command lets you display your open windows one on top of the other.

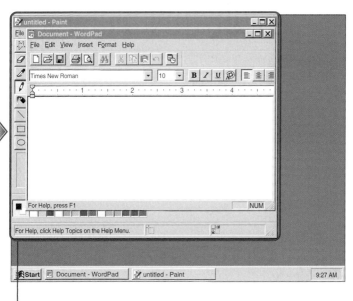

◆ The windows neatly overlap each other.

TILE WINDOWS

TILE WINDOWS

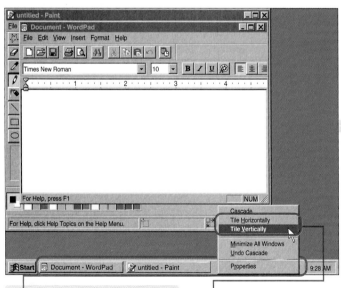

1 Move the mouse ⌖ over an empty area on the taskbar and then press the **right** button. A menu appears.

2 Move the mouse ⌖ over the Tile option you want to use and then press the left button.

You can use the Tile command to view the contents of all your open windows.

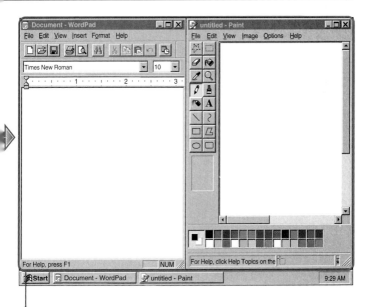

◆ You can now view the contents of all your open windows.

CLOSE A WINDOW

CLOSE A WINDOW

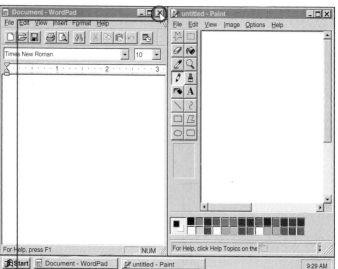

1 Move the mouse ⌖ over ⊠ in the window you want to close and then press the left button.

42

When you finish working with a window, you can close the window to remove it from your screen.

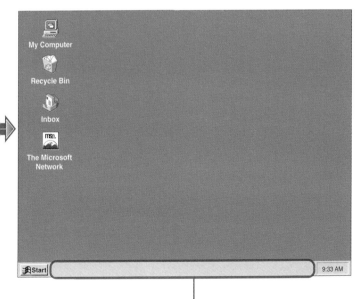

◆ The window disappears from your screen.

◆ The button for the window disappears from the taskbar.

Note: In this example, the Paint window was also closed.

43

GETTING HELP

GETTING HELP

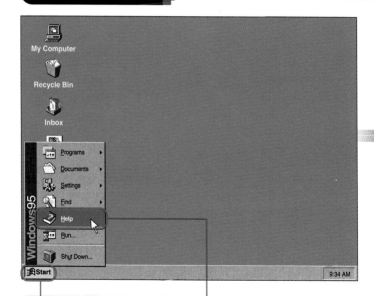

1 Move the mouse ⌖ over **Start** and then press the left button.

2 Move the mouse ⌖ over **Help** and then press the left button.

If you do not know how to perform a task, you can use the Help feature to obtain information.

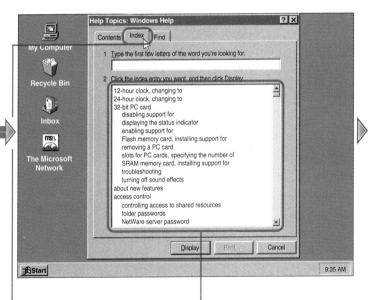

◆ The **Help Topics** window appears.

3 To display the help index, move the mouse ↖ over the **Index** tab and then press the left button.

◆ This area displays a list of all the available help topics.

45

GETTING HELP

GETTING HELP (CONTINUED)

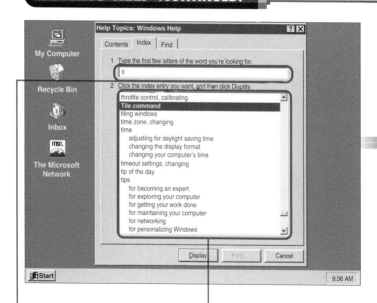

4 Move the mouse I over this area and then press the left button.

5 Type the first few letters of the topic of interest (example: **ti** for **time**).

◆ This area displays topics beginning with the letters you typed.

Note: To browse through the topics, use the scroll bar. For more information, refer to page 50.

The Help feature can save you time by eliminating the need to refer to other sources.

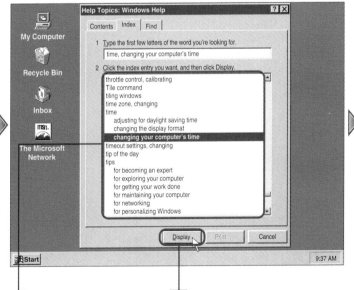

6 Move the mouse ↖ over the topic you want information on and then press the left button.

7 Move the mouse ↖ over **Display** and then press the left button.

CONTINUED

47

GETTING HELP

To save you time, the Help feature can open the dialog box that lets you perform the task you want to accomplish.

GETTING HELP (CONTINUED)

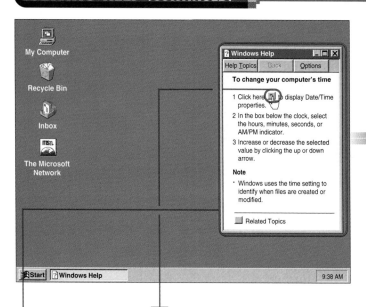

◆ Information on the topic you selected appears.

8 To open the dialog box that lets you perform the task, move the mouse 🖑 over 🔄 and then press the left button.

Note: Some help topics do not display the 🔄 button.

48

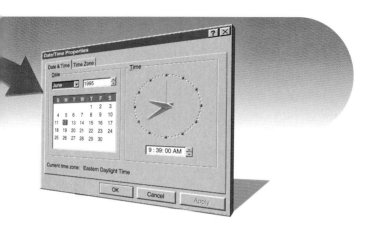

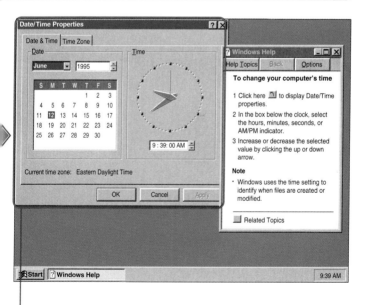

◆ In this example, the **Date/Time Properties** dialog box appears.

Note: To close a window, move the mouse ⬚ over ☒ and then press the left button.

SCROLL THROUGH A WINDOW

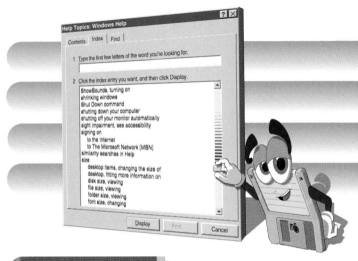

SCROLL DOWN

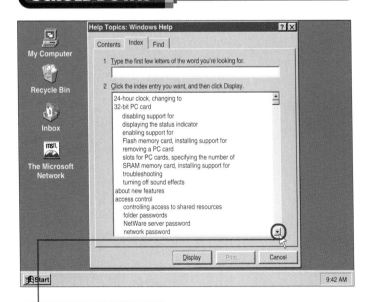

1 Move the mouse ▷ over ▾ and then press the left button.

◆ The information moves up one line, displaying a new line of information at the bottom of the window.

A scroll bar
lets you browse
through information
in a window.

SCROLL UP

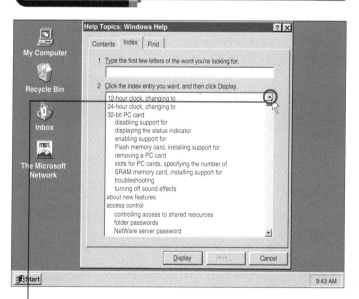

1 Move the mouse ⬡ over ▲ and then press the left button.

◆ The information moves down one line, displaying a new line of information at the top of the window.

51

SCROLL TO ANY POSITION

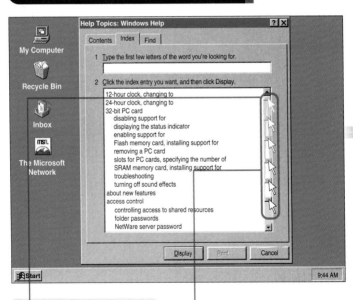

1 Move the mouse over the scroll box (▭).

2 Press and hold down the left button as you drag the scroll box along the scroll bar.

You can
scroll through a window
when the window is not large
enough to display all
the information it
contains.

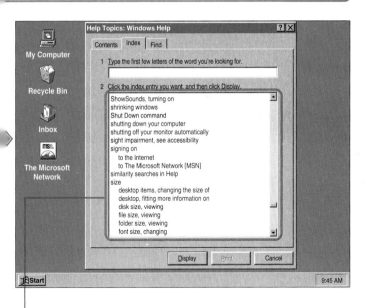

3 Release the button
when you see the
information you want.

In this chapter you will learn how to create documents quickly and efficiently using the WordPad program.

WORDPAD

Start WordPad

Enter Text

Save a Document

Exit WordPad

Open a Document

Print a Document

Select Text

Change Font Size

Change Font Type

Insert Text

Delete Text

8 point
12 point
14 point
18 point
24 point

WordPad measures the size of text in points. There are approximately 72 points in one inch.

START WORDPAD

START WORDPAD

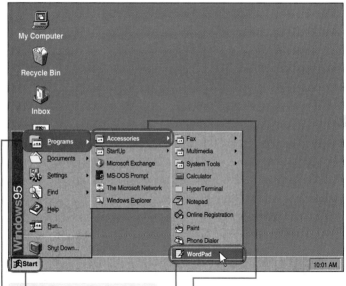

1 Move the mouse ⌖ over **Start** and then press the left button.

2 Move the mouse ⌖ over **Programs**.

3 Move the mouse ⌖ over **Accessories**.

4 Move the mouse ⌖ over **WordPad** and then press the left button.

WordPad helps you create professional-looking documents, such as letters and memos.

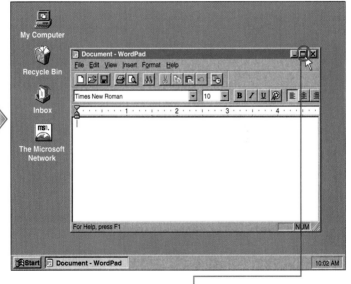

◆ The **WordPad** window appears.

5 To enlarge the **WordPad** window to fill your screen, move the mouse ▷ over ☐ and then press the left button.

ENTER TEXT

ENTER TEXT

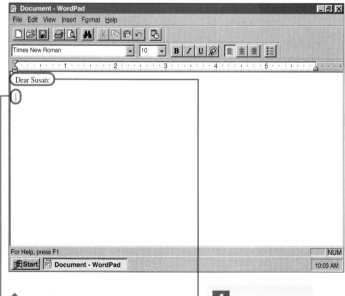

◆ The flashing line in the window is called the insertion point. It indicates where the text you type will appear.

1 Type the first line of text.

2 To start a new paragraph, press **Enter** twice.

When typing text in a document, you do not need to press **Enter** at the end of a line. WordPad automatically moves the text to the next line.

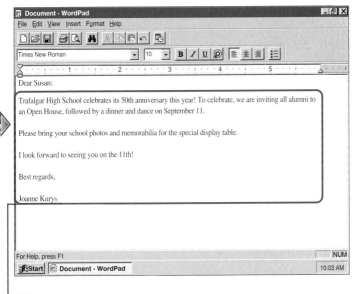

3 Type the remaining text.

◆ Press **Enter** only when you want to start a new line or paragraph.

SAVE A DOCUMENT

SAVE A DOCUMENT

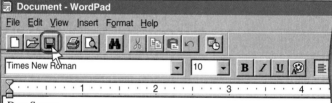

Document - WordPad

File Edit View Insert Format Help

Times New Roman   10   **B** *I* U

Dear Susan:

Trafalgar High School celebrates its 50th anniversary this year! To celebrate, an Open House, followed by a dinner and dance on September 11.

Please bring your school photos and memorabilia for the special display table.

I look forward to seeing you on the 11th!

Best regards,

1 Move the mouse over 🔲 and then press the left button.

◆ The **Save As** dialog box appears.

*Note: If you previously saved your document, the **Save As** dialog box will not appear, since you have already named the document.*

You should save your document to store it for future use. This lets you later retrieve the document for reviewing or editing purposes.

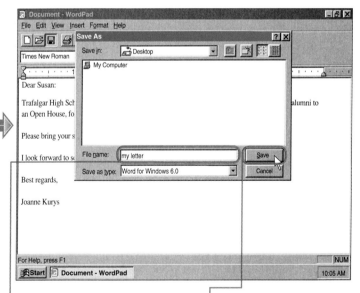

2 Type a name for your document (example: **my letter**).

*Note: You can use up to 255 characters to name a document. The name cannot contain the characters \ ? : * " < > or |.*

3 Move the mouse ⬚ over **Save** and then press the left button.

Note: To avoid losing your work, you should save your document every 5 to 10 minutes. To do so, repeat step 1.

61

EXIT WORDPAD

EXIT WORDPAD

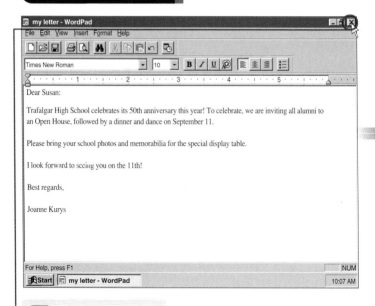

1 Move the mouse ⬚ over **X** and then press the left button.

When you finish using WordPad, you can exit the program.

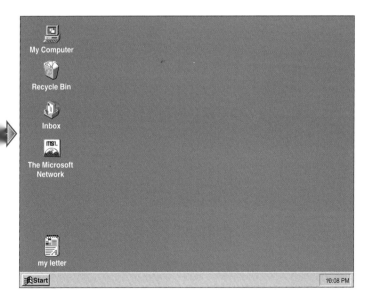

◆ The WordPad window disappears from your screen.

Note: To restart WordPad, refer to page 56.

63

OPEN A DOCUMENT

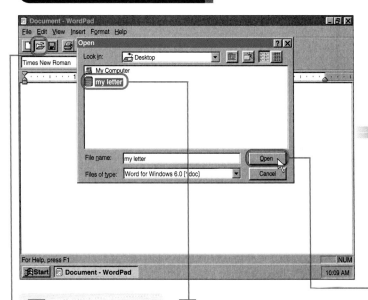

1 Move the mouse ⌖ over 📂 and then press the left button.

◆ The **Open** dialog box appears.

2 Move the mouse ⌖ over the name of the document you want to open and then press the left button.

Note: If you cannot find the document you want to open, refer to page 156 to find the document.

You can open
a saved document and
display it on your screen.
This lets you view and
make changes to the
document.

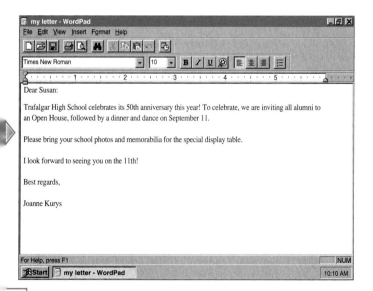

my letter - WordPad

File Edit View Insert Format Help

Times New Roman   10   **B** *I* U

Dear Susan:

Trafalgar High School celebrates its 50th anniversary this year! To celebrate, we are inviting all alumni to an Open House, followed by a dinner and dance on September 11.

Please bring your school photos and memorabilia for the special display table.

I look forward to seeing you on the 11th!

Best regards,

Joanne Kurys

For Help, press F1   NUM

Start   my letter - WordPad   10:10 AM

3 Move the mouse
over **Open** and then press
the left button.

◆ WordPad opens the
document and displays it
on your screen. You can
now review and make
changes to the document.

65

PRINT A DOCUMENT

PRINT A DOCUMENT

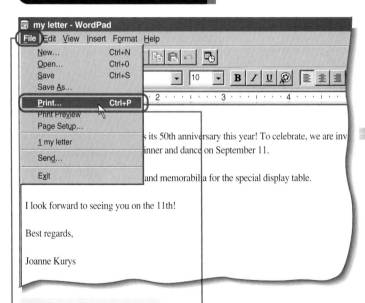

my letter - WordPad

File Edit View Insert Format Help

New...	Ctrl+N
Open...	Ctrl+O
Save	Ctrl+S
Save As...	
Print...	Ctrl+P
Print Preview	
Page Setup...	
1 my letter	
Send...	
Exit	

s its 50th anniversary this year! To celebrate, we are inv
inner and dance on September 11.

and memorabilia for the special display table.

I look forward to seeing you on the 11th!

Best regards,

Joanne Kurys

1 Move the mouse ⬚ over **File** and then press the left button.

2 Move the mouse ⬚ over **Print** and then press the left button.

66

You can produce a paper copy of the document displayed on your screen.

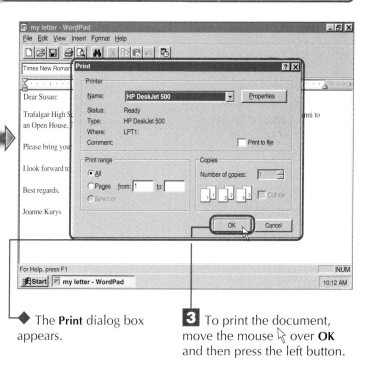

◆ The **Print** dialog box appears.

3 To print the document, move the mouse over **OK** and then press the left button.

SELECT TEXT

SELECT TEXT

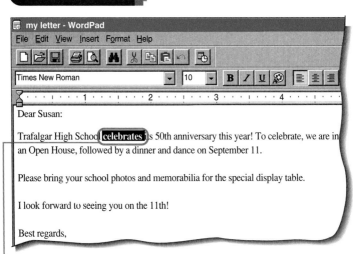

Dear Susan:

Trafalgar High School **celebrates** its 50th anniversary this year! To celebrate, we are in an Open House, followed by a dinner and dance on September 11.

Please bring your school photos and memorabilia for the special display table.

I look forward to seeing you on the 11th!

Best regards,

SELECT A WORD

1 Move the mouse I anywhere over the word you want to select and then quickly press the left button twice.

◆ To cancel a text selection, move the mouse I outside the selected area and then press the left button.

Before performing a task, you must first select the text you want to work with. Selected text appears highlighted on your screen.

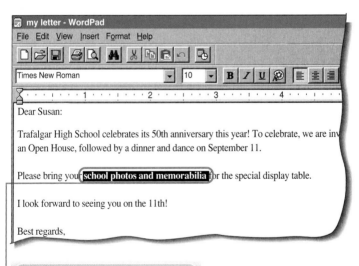

SELECT ANY AMOUNT OF TEXT

1 Move the mouse I over the first word you want to select.

2 Press and hold down the left button as you drag the mouse ⇗ over the text you want to select. Then release the button.

Note: To quickly select all the text in your document, press Ctrl + A.

69

CHANGE FONT SIZE

8 point
12 point
14 point
18 point
24 point

WordPad measures the size of text in points. There are approximately 72 points in one inch.

CHANGE FONT SIZE

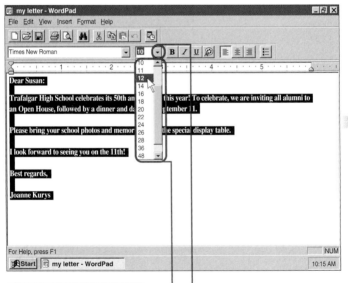

1 Select the text you want to make larger or smaller.

Note: To select text, refer to page 68.

2 Move the mouse ⌖ over ▾ in the **Font Size** box and then press the left button.

3 Move the mouse ⌖ over the size you want to use (example: **12**) and then press the left button.

You can increase or decrease the size of text in your document.

• Larger text is easier to read.

• Smaller text lets you fit more information on one page.

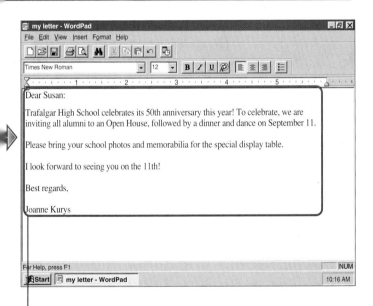

The text you selected changes to the new size.

Note: To deselect text, move the mouse I outside the selected area and then press the left button.

CHANGE FONT TYPE

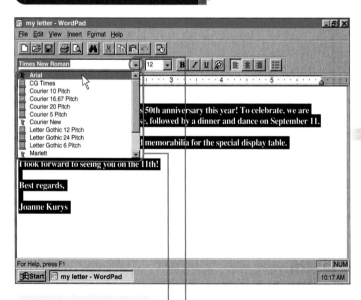

1 Select the text you want to change.

Note: To select text, refer to page 68.

2 Move the mouse ⬡ over 🔽 in the **Font** box and then press the left button.

3 Move the mouse ⬡ over the font type you want to use (example: **Arial**) and then press the left button.

72

You can enhance the appearance of your document by changing the design of characters.

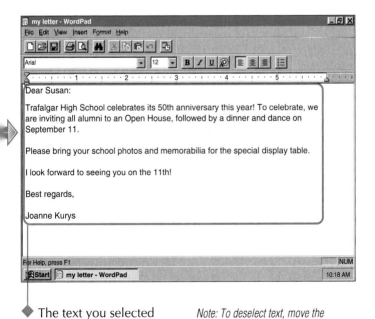

◆ The text you selected changes to the new font type.

Note: To deselect text, move the mouse I outside the selected area and then press the left button.

INSERT TEXT

You can easily add new text to your document.

INSERT TEXT

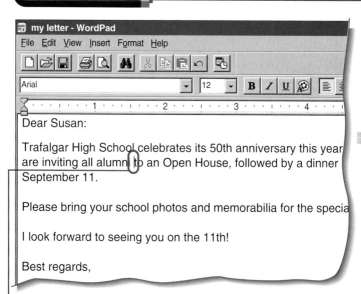

1 Move the mouse I to where you want to insert the new text and then press the left button.

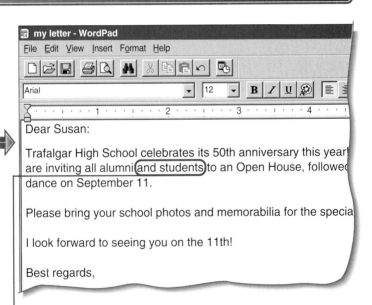

my letter - WordPad

File Edit View Insert Format Help

Arial ▾ 12 ▾ **B** *I* U 🎨 ▤ ▤

Dear Susan:

Trafalgar High School celebrates its 50th anniversary this year! are inviting all alumni and students to an Open House, followed dance on September 11.

Please bring your school photos and memorabilia for the specia

I look forward to seeing you on the 11th!

Best regards,

2 Type the text you want to insert.

Note: The words to the right of the new text move forward.

3 To insert a blank space, press the **Spacebar**.

75

DELETE TEXT

DELETE TEXT

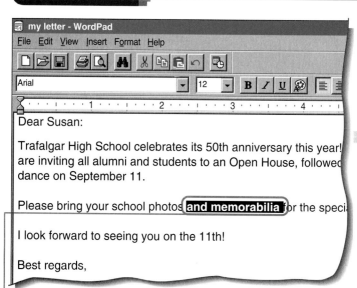

my letter - WordPad

File Edit View Insert Format Help

Arial   12   **B** *I* U

Dear Susan:

Trafalgar High School celebrates its 50th anniversary this year!
are inviting all alumni and students to an Open House, followed
dance on September 11.

Please bring your school photos **and memorabilia** for the specia

I look forward to seeing you on the 11th!

Best regards,

1 Select the text you
want to delete.

*Note: To select text, refer
to page 68.*

76

You can easily
remove text you no
longer need.

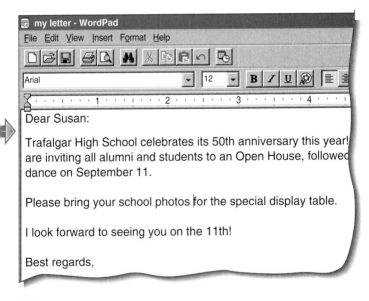

my letter - WordPad

File Edit View Insert Format Help

Arial   ▼   12   ▼   **B** *I* <u>U</u> 🎨 ≣ ≣

· · · · 1 · · · · 2 · · · · 3 · · · · 4 · · · ·

Dear Susan:

Trafalgar High School celebrates its 50th anniversary this year!
are inviting all alumni and students to an Open House, followed
dance on September 11.

Please bring your school photos for the special display table.

I look forward to seeing you on the 11th!

Best regards,

2 Press Delete on your
keyboard to remove
the text.

PAINT

START PAINT

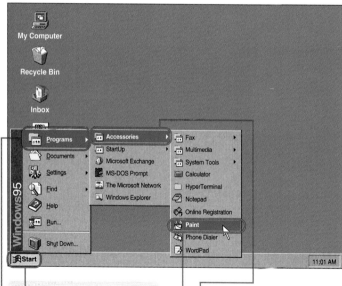

1 Move the mouse ⌖ over **Start** and then press the left button.

2 Move the mouse ⌖ over **Programs**.

3 Move the mouse ⌖ over **Accessories**.

4 Move the mouse ⌖ over **Paint** and then press the left button.

Paint lets you use your artistic abilities to draw pictures and maps on your computer.

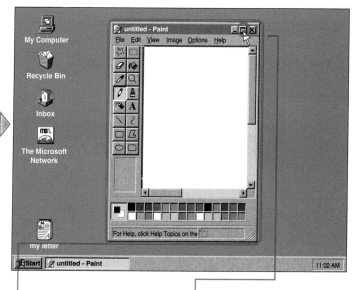

◆ The **Paint** window appears.

5 To enlarge the window to fill your screen, move the mouse ℝ over ▣ and then press the left button.

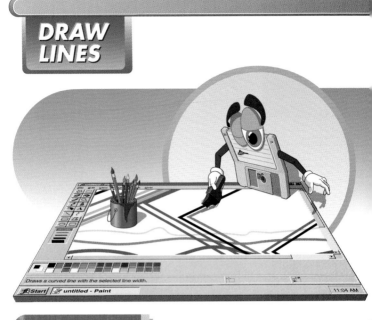

DRAW LINES

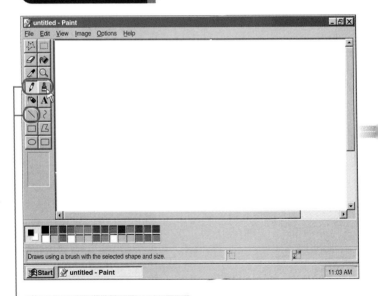

1 Move the mouse ▷ over the line tool you want to use (example: 📐) and then press the left button.

🖊	Draws thin, wavy lines.
📐	Draws wavy lines of different thicknesses.
◹	Draws straight lines of different thicknesses.

82

You can draw straight or wavy lines in any color displayed at the bottom of your screen.

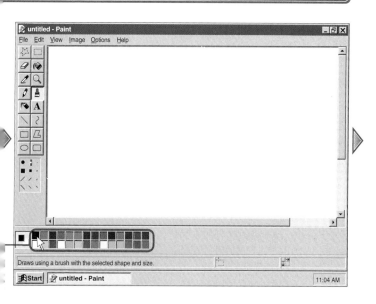

Draws using a brush with the selected shape and size.

Start 🖉 untitled - Paint   11:04 AM

2 To select a color for the line, move the mouse ▷ over the color (example: ■) and then press the left button.

CONTINUED

You can select a different thickness for your line.

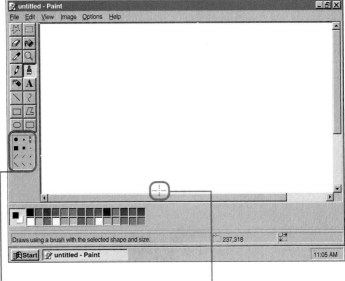

3 To select a line thickness, move the mouse ⬭ over one of these options and then press the left button.

Note: The tool does not provide any line thickness options.

4 Move the mouse ⬭ to where you want to begin drawing the line and ⬭ changes to ┼ or ∂.

84

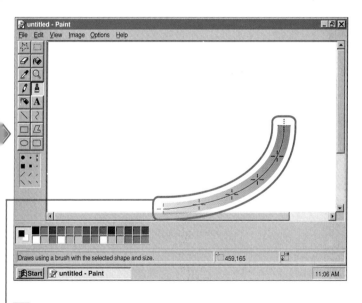

5 Press and hold down the left button as you move the mouse ┼ until the line is the length you want. Then release the button.

Note: When using the ◥ or ✏ tool, you can draw a perfectly horizontal, vertical or 45-degree line. To do so, press and hold down `Shift` *before and during step* **5** *.*

DRAW SHAPES

Paint offers these options for creating shapes.

DRAW SHAPES

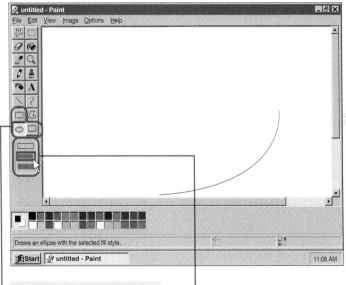

1 Move the mouse ⌖ over the tool displaying the shape you want to draw (example: ⬭) and then press the left button.

2 To select how you want the shape to appear, move the mouse ⌖ over one of these options and then press the left button.

Note: For more information, refer to the top of page 87.

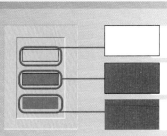

Draws the outline of a shape.

Draws the outline of a shape and fills the inside with color.

Draws a colored shape with no outline.

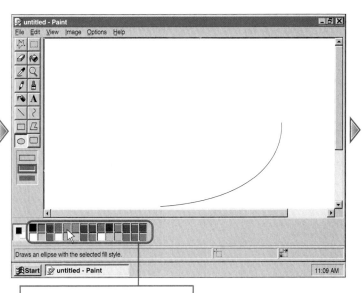

3 To select a color for the outline of the shape, move the mouse ⬚ over the color (example: ■) and then press the left button.

4 To select a color for the inside of the shape, move the mouse ⬚ over the color (example: ■) and then press the **right** button.

CONTINUED

87

DRAW SHAPES (CONTINUED)

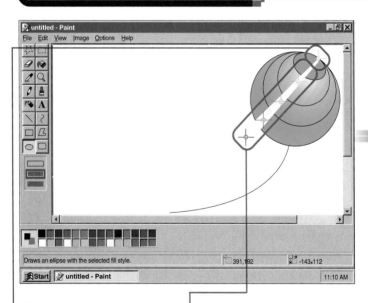

Draws an ellipse with the selected fill style.

5 Move the mouse ⬉ to where you want to begin drawing the shape and ⬉ changes to ─╬─.

6 Press and hold down the left button as you drag the shape to the size you want. Then release the button.

Note: To draw a perfect circle or square, press and hold down **Shift** *before and during step* **6**.

88

You can draw circles and squares to complete your drawing.

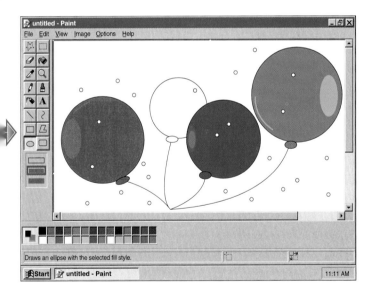

◆ You can now use the shape and line tools to complete your drawing.

Note: For information on drawing lines, refer to page 82.

Note: To print the drawing, perform steps **1** *to* **3** *starting on page 66.*

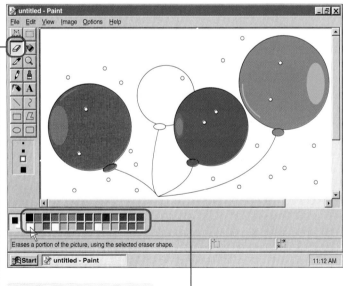

1 Move the mouse ⌖ over 🖉 and then press the left button.

2 To select a color for the eraser, move the mouse ⌖ over the color (example: ☐) and then press the **right** button.

You can use the Eraser tool to remove part of your drawing.

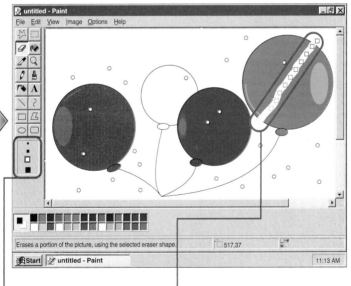

Erases a portion of the picture, using the selected eraser shape. 517,37

Start untitled - Paint   11:13 AM

3 Move the mouse ⤴ over the eraser size you want to use and then press the left button.

4 Move the mouse ⤴ to where you want to start erasing (⤴ changes to ☐).

5 Press and hold down the left button as you move the mouse ☐ over the area you want to erase. Then release the button.

91

UNDO LAST CHANGE

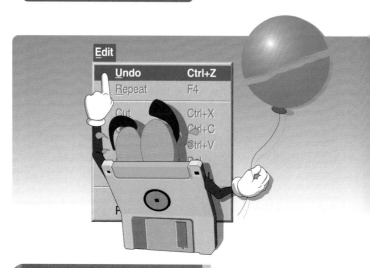

UNDO LAST CHANGE

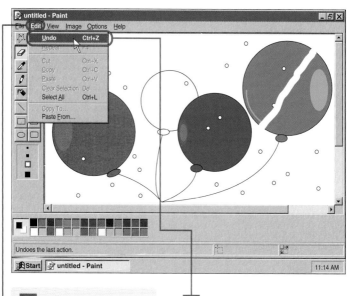

1 Move the mouse ⟂ over **Edit** and then press the left button.

2 Move the mouse ⟂ over **Undo** and then press the left button.

Paint remembers the last change you made to your drawing. If you regret this change, you can cancel it by using the Undo feature.

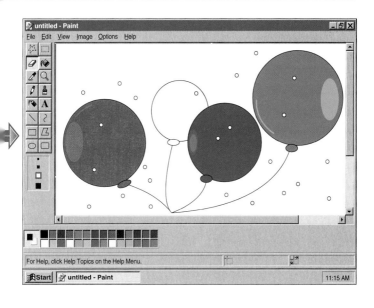

◆ Paint cancels the last change you made to the drawing.

SAVE A DRAWING

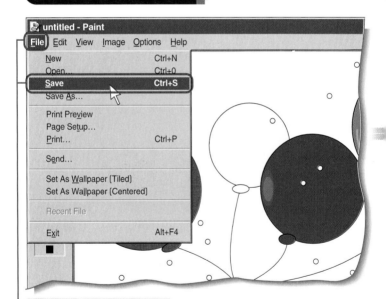

1 Move the mouse 🖰 over **File** and then press the left button.

2 Move the mouse 🖰 over **Save** and then press the left button.

◆ The **Save As** dialog box appears.

*Note: If you previously saved your drawing, the **Save As** dialog box will not appear, since you have already named the drawing.*

94

You should save your drawing to store it for future use. This lets you later review and make changes to the drawing.

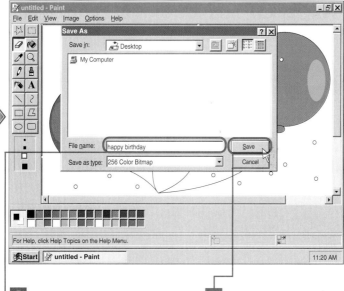

3 Type a name for your drawing.

*Note: You can use up to 255 characters to name your drawing. The name cannot contain the characters \ ? : * " < > or |.*

4 Move the mouse over **Save** and then press the left button.

*Note: To avoid losing your work, you should save your drawing every 5 to 10 minutes. To do so, repeat steps **1** and **2**.*

95

EXIT PAINT

When you finish using Paint, you can exit the program.

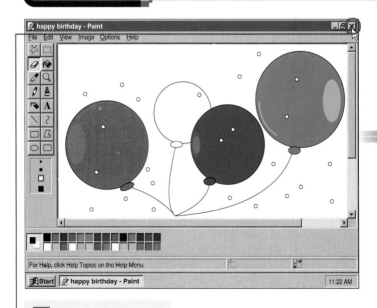

1 Move the mouse ⃗ over ☒ and then press the left button.

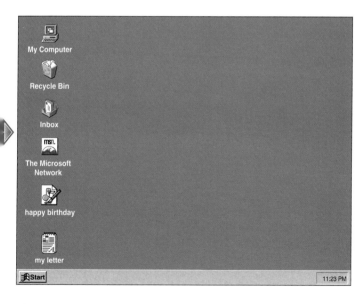

◆ The Paint window disappears from your screen.

Note: To restart Paint, refer to page 80.

OPEN A DRAWING

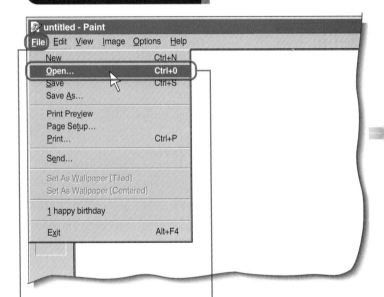

◆ To start **Paint**, refer to page 80.

1 Move the mouse ↖ over **File** and then press the left button.

2 Move the mouse ↖ over **Open** and then press the left button.

◆ The **Open** dialog box appears.

98

You can open a saved drawing and display it on your screen.

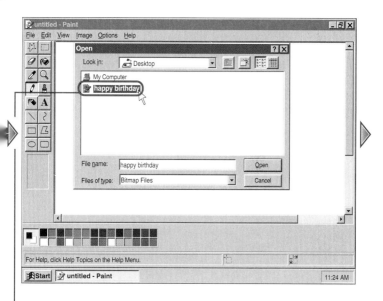

3 Move the mouse ↖ over the name of the drawing you want to open and then press the left button.

Note: If you cannot find the drawing you want to open, refer to page 156 to find the drawing.

CONTINUED

OPEN A DRAWING (CONTINUED)

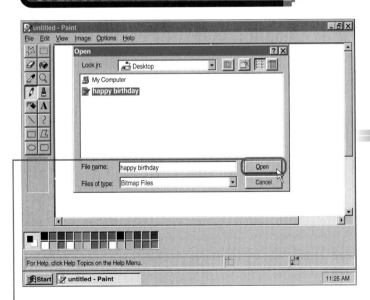

4 Move the mouse ↕ over **Open** and then press the left button.

After opening
a drawing, you
can view and make
changes to the
drawing.

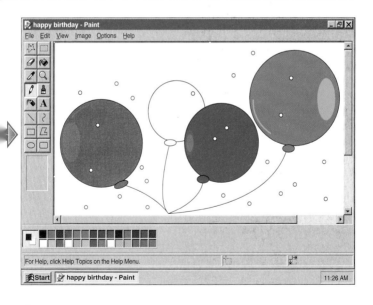

◆ Paint opens the drawing
and displays it on your screen.
You can now review and make
changes to the drawing.

101

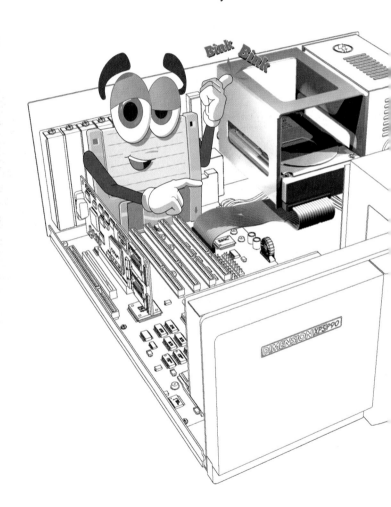

VIEW CONTENTS OF COMPUTER

STORAGE DEVICES

The hard drive is the primary device that a computer uses to store information.

Most computers come with one hard drive, located inside the computer case. It is called drive C.

FLOPPY DRIVE (A:)

A floppy drive stores and retrieves information on floppy disks (diskettes). If your computer has only one floppy drive, it is called drive A. If your computer has two floppy drives, the second drive is called drive B.

CD-ROM DRIVE (D:)

A CD-ROM drive is a device that reads information stored on compact discs. You cannot change information stored on a compact disc.

Note: Your computer may not have a CD-ROM drive.

VIEW CONTENTS OF COMPUTER

Like a filing cabinet, your computer uses folders to organize information.

VIEW CONTENTS OF COMPUTER

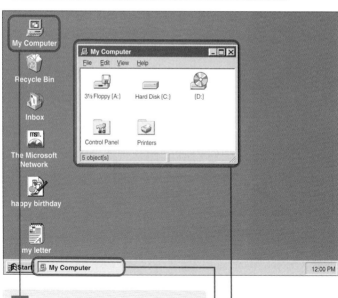

1 To view the contents of your computer, move the mouse over **My Computer** and then quickly press the left button twice.

◆ The **My Computer** window opens.

◆ The taskbar displays the name of the opened window.

You can easily view the folders and files stored on your computer.

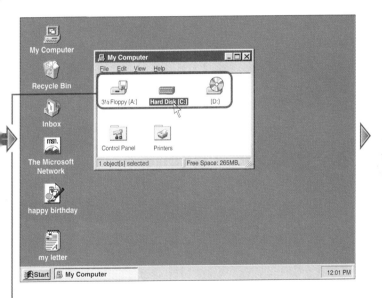

◆ These objects represent the drives on your computer.

2 To display the contents of a drive, move the mouse ⌖ over the drive (example: **C:**) and then quickly press the left button twice.

*Note: If you want to view the contents of a floppy or CD-ROM drive, make sure you insert a floppy disk or CD-ROM disc before performing step **2**.*

CONTINUED

107

A window on your screen can display folders and files.

VIEW CONTENTS (CONTINUED)

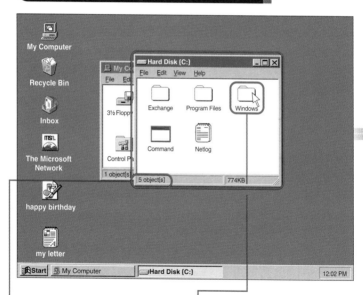

◆ A window appears, displaying the contents of the drive.

◆ This area tells you how many objects are in the window.

3 To display the contents of a folder, move the mouse ⅄ over the folder (example: **Windows**) and then quickly press the left button twice.

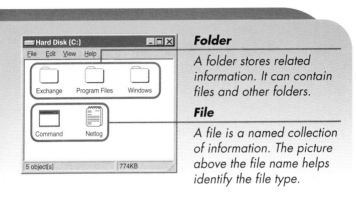

Folder

A folder stores related information. It can contain files and other folders.

File

A file is a named collection of information. The picture above the file name helps identify the file type.

◆ A new window appears, displaying the contents of the folder.

CHANGE SIZE OF ITEMS

CHANGE SIZE OF ITEMS

1 Move the mouse ↖ over **View** and then press the left button.

2 To enlarge the items in a window, move the mouse ↖ over **Large Icons** and then press the left button.

110

You can change the size of items displayed in a window. Enlarging items lets you view the items more clearly.

◆ The items change to a larger size.

*Note: To return to the smaller item size, repeat steps 1 and 2, selecting **Small Icons** in step 2.*

ARRANGE ITEMS

You can have Windows automatically arrange items to fit in a window.

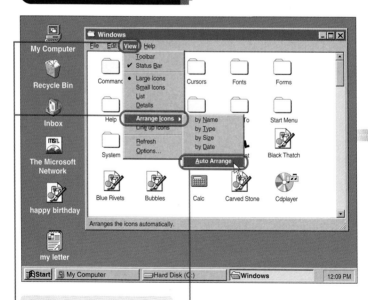

1 Move the mouse � over **View** and then press the left button.

2 Move the mouse � over **Arrange Icons**.

3 To turn on Auto Arrange, move the mouse � over **Auto Arrange** and then press the left button.

Note: If this area displays a check mark (✔), Auto Arrange is on. To leave the feature on, press **Alt** *on your keyboard.*

If you change the size of a window when the Auto Arrange feature is on, Windows will automatically rearrange the items to fit the new size.

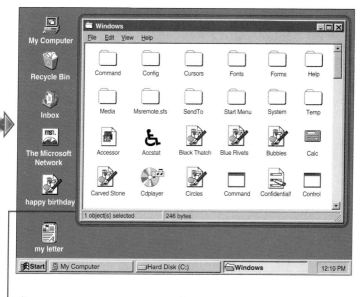

◆ The items fit in the window.

◆ To turn off Auto Arrange, repeat steps **1** to **3**.

DISPLAY FILE INFORMATION

DISPLAY FILE INFORMATION

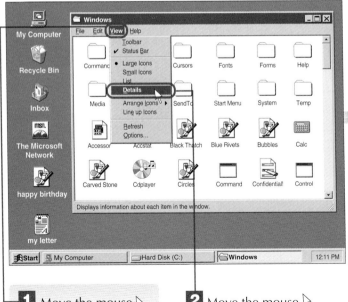

1 Move the mouse ⌕ over **View** and then press the left button.

2 Move the mouse ⌕ over **Details** and then press the left button.

114

Windows lets you display information about the files listed in a window.

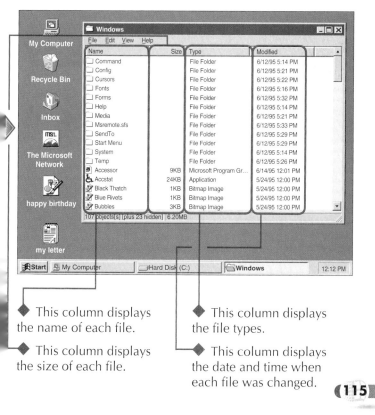

◆ This column displays the name of each file.

◆ This column displays the size of each file.

◆ This column displays the file types.

◆ This column displays the date and time when each file was changed.

DISPLAY FILE NAMES ONLY

DISPLAY FILE NAMES ONLY

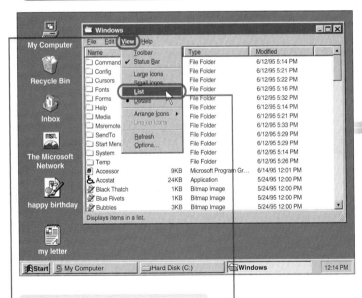

1 To hide the file information and display only the file names, move the mouse ⌖ over **View** and then press the left button.

2 Move the mouse ⌖ over **List** and then press the left button.

You can hide
the file information
and display only
the file names.

◆ Only the file names are
displayed on your screen.

SORT ITEMS

NAME   SIZE
SORT ITEMS   SORT ITEMS

SORT BY NAME

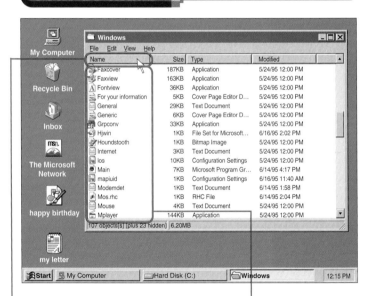

1 To sort the item names from A to Z, move the mouse over **Name** and then press the left button.

*Note: If the **Name** button is not displayed, perform steps* **1** *and* **2** *on page 114.*

◆ The items in the window are sorted.

Note: To sort the item names from Z to A, repeat step **1**.

118

You can sort the items displayed in a window by name or size.

SORT BY SIZE

1 To sort the items from smallest to largest, move the mouse ⫣ over **Size** and then press the left button.

*Note: If the **Size** button is not displayed, perform steps **1** and **2** on page 114.*

◆ The items in the window are sorted.

*Note: To sort the items from largest to smallest, repeat step **1**.*

119

SORT ITEMS

SORT BY TYPE

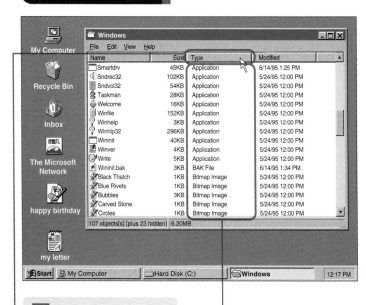

1 To sort the item types from A to Z, move the mouse ⍟ over **Type** and then press the left button.

*Note: If the **Type** button is not displayed, perform steps **1** and **2** on page 114.*

◆ The items in the window are sorted.

*Note: To sort the item types from Z to A, repeat step **1**.*

120

You can also
sort the items
displayed in a window
by type or date.

SORT BY DATE

1 To sort the items from
newest to oldest, move the
mouse ▷ over **Modified** and
then press the left button.

*Note: If the **Modified** button is not
displayed, perform steps 1 and 2
on page 114.*

◆ The items in the
window are sorted.

*Note: To sort the items from
oldest to newest, repeat step 1.*

In this chapter you will learn how to work with files stored on your computer.

WORK WITH FILES

Select Files

Create a New Folder

Move a File to a Folder

Copy a File to a Floppy Disk

Rename a File

Open a File

Open a Recently Used File

Print a File

Delete a File

Restore a Deleted File

Find a File

SELECT A FILE

1 Move the mouse ↕ over the file you want to select and then press the left button.

◆ The file is highlighted.

Note: To deselect files, move the mouse ↕ over a blank area in the window and then press the left button.

Before working
with a file, you must
select the file you want to
work with. Selected files
appear highlighted
on your screen.

◆ This area displays
the number of files
you selected.

◆ This area displays the total
size of the files you selected.

*Note: One byte equals one character. One
kilobyte (KB) equals approximately one
page of double spaced text.*

125

SELECT FILES

SELECT A GROUP OF FILES

1 Move the mouse ⌖ over the first file you want to select and then press the left button.

2 Press and hold down **Shift** on your keyboard.

3 Still holding down **Shift**, move the mouse ⌖ over the last file you want to select and then press the left button.

Windows lets you easily select multiple files. This lets you work with several files at the same time.

SELECT ANY FILES

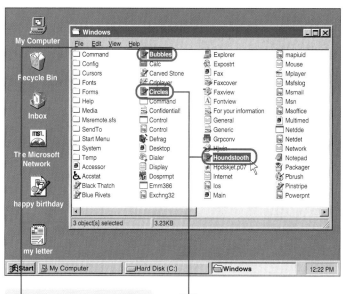

1 Move the mouse ⌖ over a file you want to select and then press the left button.

2 Press and hold down Ctrl on your keyboard.

3 Still holding down Ctrl, repeat step **1** for each file you want to select.

127

CREATE A NEW FOLDER

1 Display the contents of the drive or folder where you want to place the new folder.

Note: For more information, refer to page 106.

2 To deselect any selected files, move the mouse ⬉ over a blank area in the window and then press the left button.

3 Move the mouse ⬉ over **File** and then press the left button.

128

You can create a new folder to better organize the information stored on your computer.

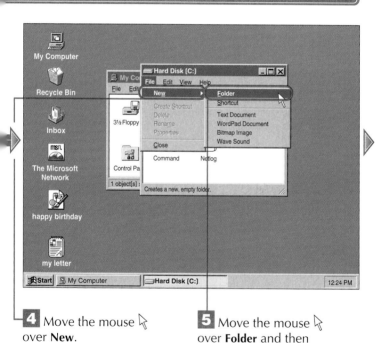

4 Move the mouse ⬡ over **New**.

5 Move the mouse ⬡ over **Folder** and then press the left button.

CONTINUED

CREATE A NEW FOLDER

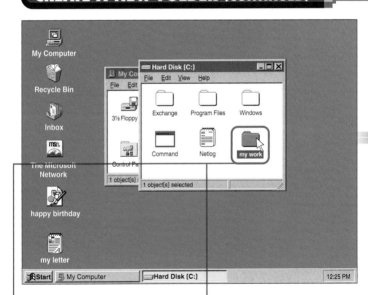

◆ The new folder appears, displaying a temporary name (New Folder).

6 Type a name for the new folder (example: **my work**) and then press Enter.

7 To display the contents of the new folder, move the mouse ▷ over the folder and then quickly press the left button twice.

130

Creating a folder is like placing a new folder in a filing cabinet.

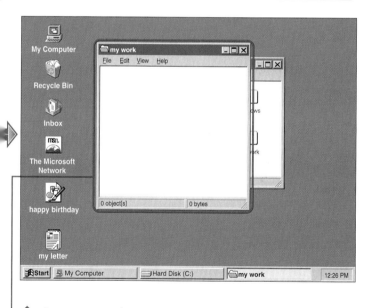

◆ The contents of the folder appear.

Note: To close a window, move the mouse ▷ over ☒ and then press the left button.

131

MOVE A FILE TO A FOLDER

MOVE A FILE TO A FOLDER

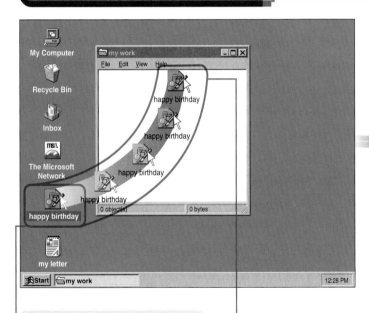

1 Position the mouse ⬚ over the file you want to move.

Note: To move more than one file, select the files. To select multiple files, refer to page 126.

2 Press and hold down the left button as you drag the mouse ⬚ to where you want to place the file.

You can reorganize the files stored on your computer by placing them in different folders.

Moving files is similar to rearranging documents in a filing cabinet to make them easier to find.

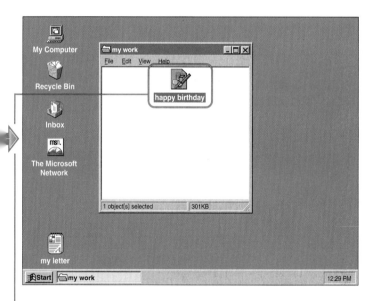

3 Release the button and the file moves to the new location.

COPY A FILE TO A FOLDER

To copy a file, perform steps **1** to **3**, except press and hold down Ctrl on your keyboard before and during step **3**.

133

COPY A FILE TO A FLOPPY DISK

1 Insert a floppy disk into a drive.

You can make an exact copy of a file and then place the copy on a floppy disk.

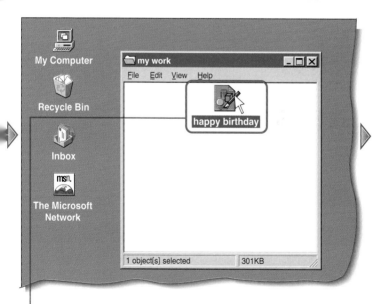

2 To select the file you want to copy, move the mouse ⌖ over the file and then press the left button.

Note: To copy more than one file, select the files. To select multiple files, refer to page 126.

COPY A FILE TO A FLOPPY DISK

COPY FILE TO DISK (CONTINUED)

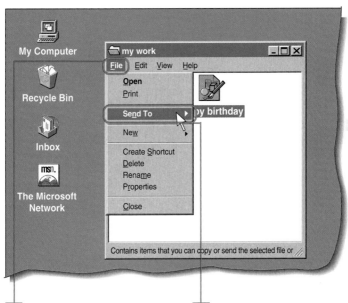

3 Move the mouse ⬚ over **File** and then press the left button.

4 Move the mouse ⬚ over **Send To**.

Copying a file to a floppy disk is useful if you want to give a copy of the file to a colleague.

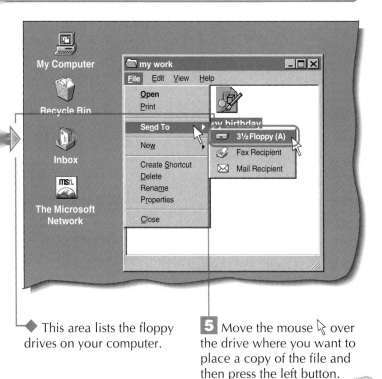

◆ This area lists the floppy drives on your computer.

5 Move the mouse ⬡ over the drive where you want to place a copy of the file and then press the left button.

RENAME A FILE

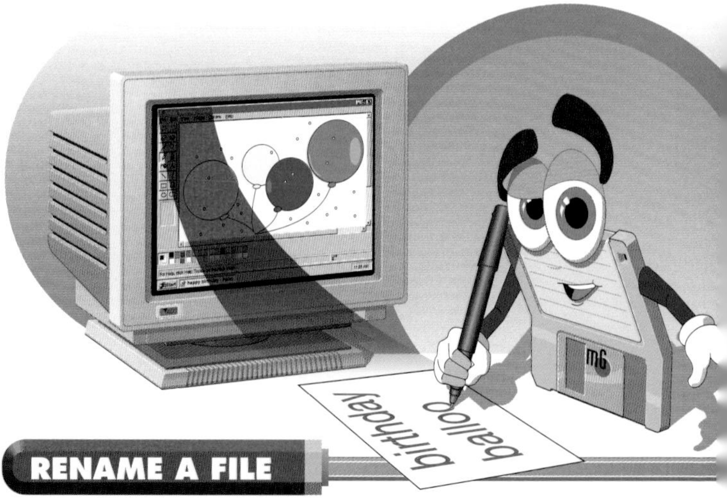

RENAME A FILE

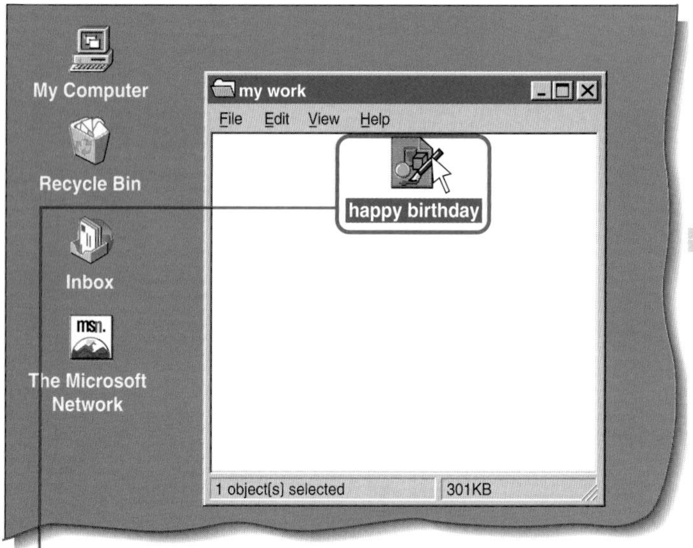

1 To select the file you want to rename, move the mouse over the file and then press the left button.

You can give
a file a new name to
better describe its
contents.

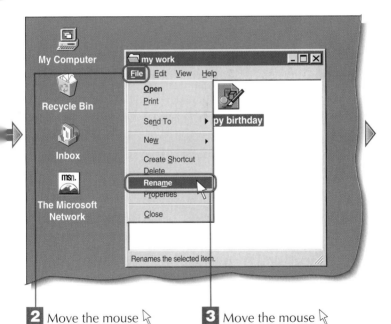

2 Move the mouse ⌖ over **File** and then press the left button.

3 Move the mouse ⌖ over **Rename** and then press the left button.

CONTINUED

139

RENAME A FILE

RENAME A FILE (CONTINUED)

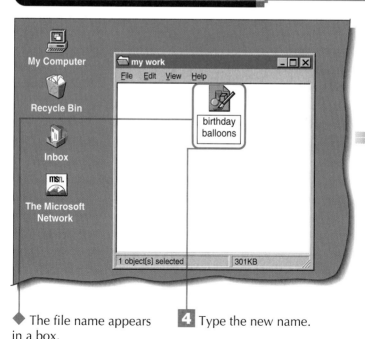

◆ The file name appears in a box.

4 Type the new name.

*Note: You can use up to 255 characters to name a file. The name cannot contain the characters \ ? : * " < > or |.*

140

Renaming a file
can make it easier
to find the file.

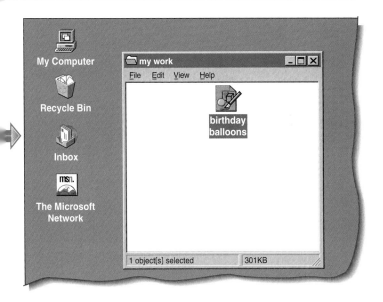

5 Press **Enter** on
your keyboard.

OPEN A FILE

You can open a file to display its contents on your screen. This lets you view and make changes to the file.

OPEN A FILE

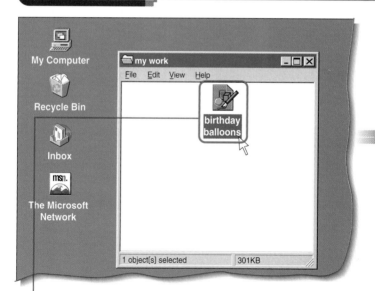

1 Move the mouse ⌖ over the file you want to open and then quickly press the left button twice.

142

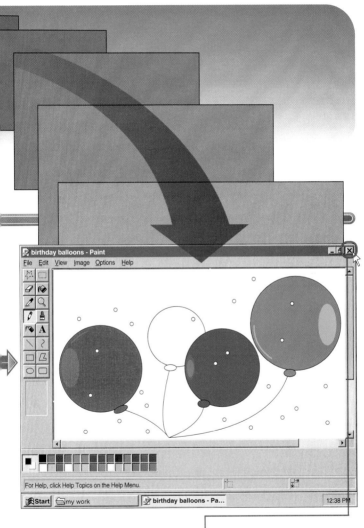

◆ The file opens. You can review and make changes to the file.

2 To close the file, move the mouse ⌖ over **X** and then press the left button.

143

OPEN A RECENTLY USED FILE

OPEN A RECENTLY USED FILE

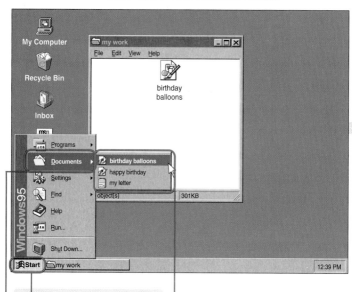

1 Move the mouse ⬚ over **Start** and then press the left button.

2 Move the mouse ⬚ over **Documents**.

◆ A list of the files you most recently used appears.

Note: Some files may not appear in this list.

3 Move the mouse ⬚ over the file you want to open and then press the left button.

144

Windows
remembers the files
you most recently used.
You can quickly open
one of these
files.

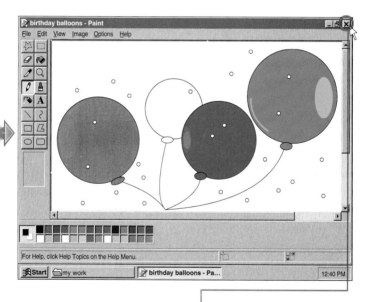

◆ The file opens. You can review and make changes to the file.

4 To close the file, move the mouse ▷ over ✕ and then press the left button.

145

PRINT A FILE

PRINT A FILE

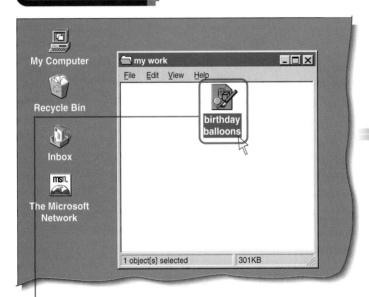

1 To select the file you want to print, move the mouse ⌖ over the file and then press the left button.

Note: To print more than one file, select the files. To select multiple files, refer to page 126.

146

You can produce a paper copy of a file stored on your computer.

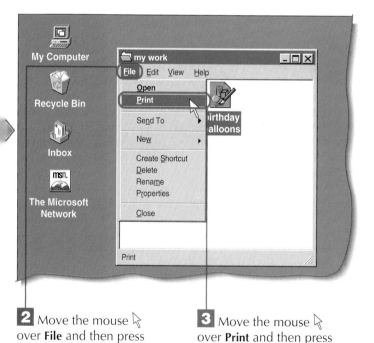

2 Move the mouse ⌖ over **File** and then press the left button.

3 Move the mouse ⌖ over **Print** and then press the left button.

DELETE A FILE

DELETE A FILE

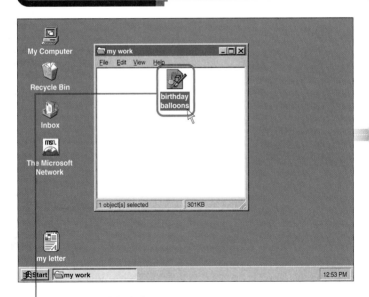

1 To select the file you want to delete, move the mouse ⌖ over the file and then press the left button.

Note: To delete more than one file, select the files. To select multiple files, refer to page 126.

You can
delete a file that
you no longer
need.

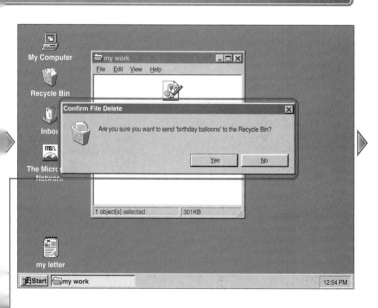

2 Press Delete on your
keyboard and the **Confirm File
Delete** dialog box appears.

CONTINUED

149

DELETE A FILE

DELETE A FILE (CONTINUED)

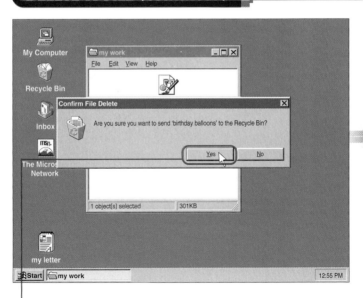

3 To delete the file, move the mouse ⌖ over **Yes** and then press the left button.

> Make sure
> you do not delete
> files you may need
> in the future.

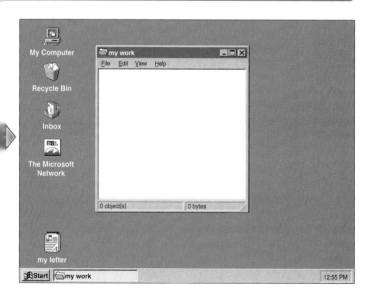

◆ The file disappears.

Note: To close a window, refer to page 42.

◆ If you delete a file you need, you can restore the file.

Note: For more information, refer to page 152.

RESTORE A DELETED FILE

RESTORE A DELETED FILE

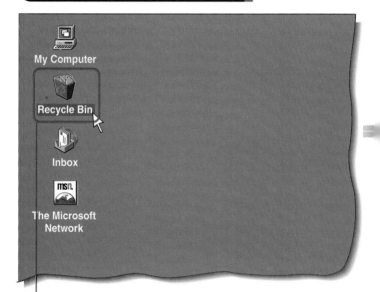

My Computer

Recycle Bin

Inbox

msn.
The Microsoft
Network

1 To display all the files you have deleted, move the mouse ⌖ over **Recycle Bin** and then quickly press the left button twice.

The Recycle Bin stores all the files you have deleted. You can easily restore any of these files.

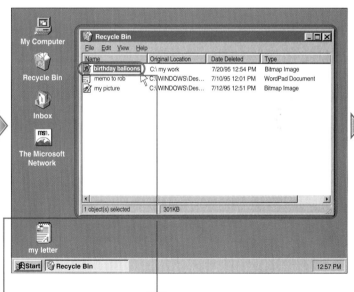

◆ The **Recycle Bin** window appears, listing all the files you have deleted.

2 To select the file you want to restore, move the mouse ⬛ over the file and then press the left button.

CONTINUED

153

RESTORE A DELETED FILE

The appearance of the Recycle Bin indicates whether the bin contains deleted files.

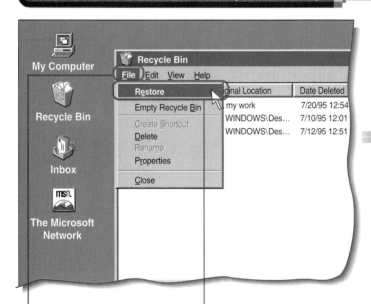

My Computer

Recycle Bin

Inbox

msn.
The Microsoft Network

Recycle Bin		
File Edit View Help		
Restore	ginal Location	Date Deleted
Empty Recycle Bin	my work	7/20/95 12:54
Create Shortcut	WINDOWS\Des…	7/10/95 12:01
Delete	WINDOWS\Des…	7/12/95 12:51
Rename		
Properties		
Close		

3 Move the mouse ⟋ over **File** and then press the left button.

4 Move the mouse ⟋ over **Restore** and then press the left button.

154

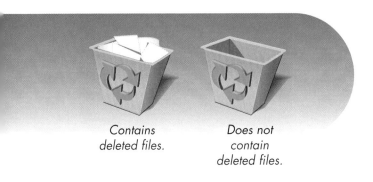

Contains
deleted files.

Does not
contain
deleted files.

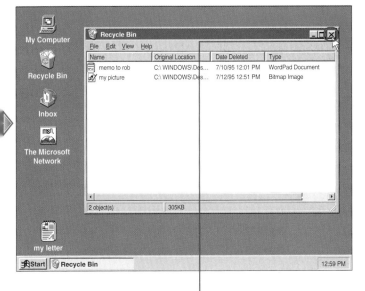

◆ The file disappears
from the list. Windows
places the file back in its
original location.

5 To close the **Recycle Bin**
window, move the mouse ⌖
over ⊠ and then press the
left button.

FIND A FILE

FIND A FILE

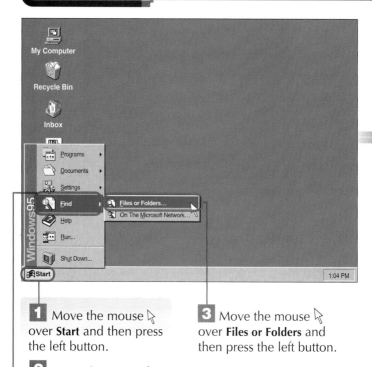

1 Move the mouse ⌖ over **Start** and then press the left button.

2 Move the mouse ⌖ over **Find**.

3 Move the mouse ⌖ over **Files or Folders** and then press the left button.

156

If you cannot remember the name or location of a file you want to work with, you can have Windows search for the file.

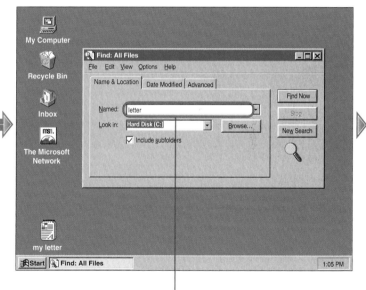

◆ The **Find: All Files** dialog box appears.

4 If you know all or part of the name of the file you want to find, type the name (example: **letter**).

CONTINUED

157

FIND A FILE

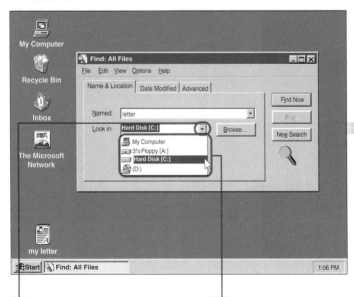

5 To specify where you want Windows to search for the file, move the mouse ⬐ over ▾ in the **Look in:** box and then press the left button.

6 Move the mouse ⬐ over the location you want to search and then press the left button.

You must specify the location you want Windows to search for the file.

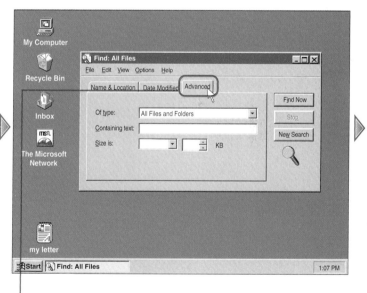

7 If you know a word or phrase in the file you want to find, move the mouse ⬉ over the **Advanced** tab and then press the left button.

*Note: If you do not know a word or phrase in the file, skip to step **9**.*

CONTINUED

159

FIND A FILE

FIND A FILE (CONTINUED)

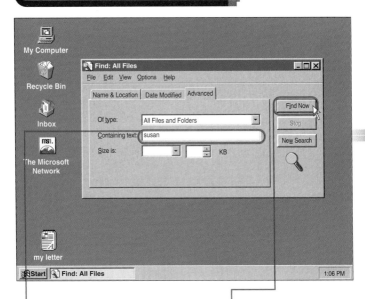

8 Move the mouse I over the box beside **Containing text:** and then press the left button. Type the word or phrase (example: **susan**).

9 To start the search, move the mouse ⌖ over **Find Now** and then press the left button.

160

When the search is complete, Windows displays a list of the files it found. You can open any of these files.

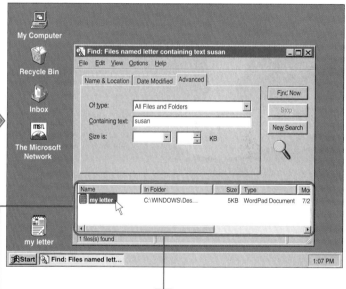

◆ This area displays the names of the files Windows found and information about each file.

10 To open a file, move the mouse ⥾ over the name of the file and then quickly press the left button twice.

Note: To close a window, move the mouse ⥾ over ✕ and then press the left button.

161

In this chapter you will learn how to customize the Windows screen to suit your needs. You will also learn how to change the date and the way the mouse works.

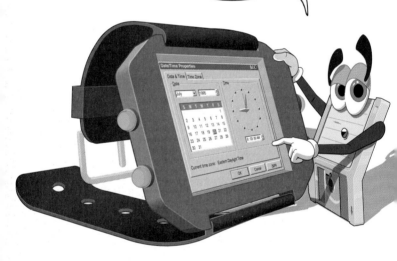

CHANGE WINDOWS SETTINGS

Change the Date and Time

Add Wallpaper

Change Screen Colors

Set Up a Screen Saver

Change Mouse Settings

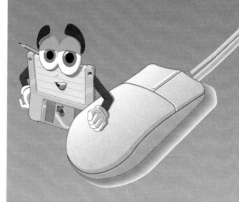

CHANGE THE DATE AND TIME

CHANGE THE DATE AND TIME

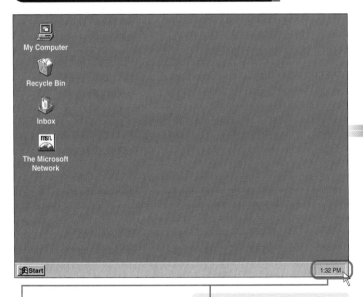

◆ This area displays the time set in your computer.

1 To change the date or time, move the mouse ⬚ over this area and then quickly press the left button twice.

You can easily
change the date and time
set in your computer.

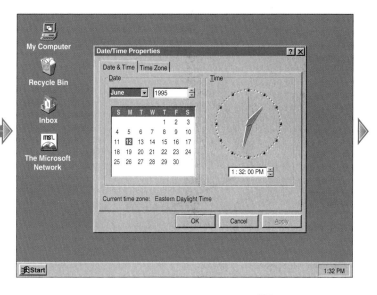

The **Date/Time Properties** dialog box appears.

CONTINUED

CHANGE THE DATE AND TIME

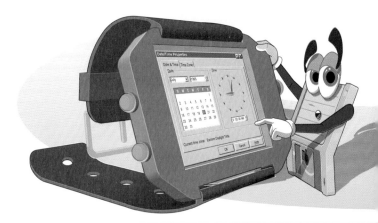

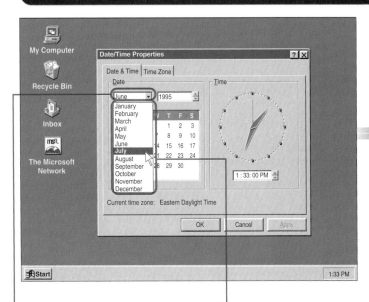

◆ This area displays the month set in your computer.

2 To change the month, move the mouse ⊠ over this area and then press the left button.

3 Move the mouse ⊠ over the correct month (example: **July**) and then press the left button.

166

It is important to have the correct date and time set in your computer. Windows uses this information to identify each document you create or update.

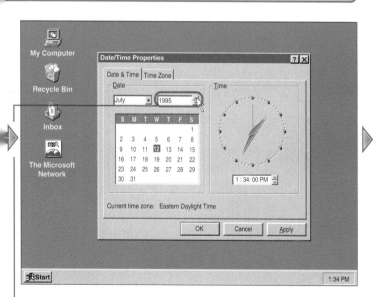

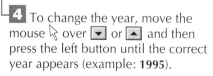

◆ This area displays the year set in your computer.

4 To change the year, move the mouse ⬡ over ▼ or ▲ and then press the left button until the correct year appears (example: **1995**).

CONTINUED

CHANGE THE DATE AND TIME

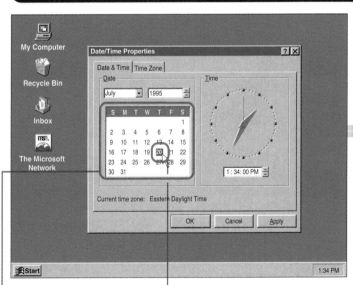

◆ This area displays the days in the month. The current day is highlighted.

5 To change the day, move the mouse ▷ over the correct day (example: **20**) and then press the left button.

168

A computer has a built-in clock that keeps track of the date and time even when you turn off the computer.

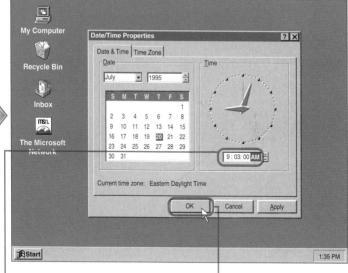

◆ This area displays the time set in your computer.

6 To change the time, move the mouse I over the part of the time you want to change and then quickly press the left button twice. Then type the correct information.

7 To apply the date and time changes you made, move the mouse over **OK** and then press the left button.

169

ADD WALLPAPER

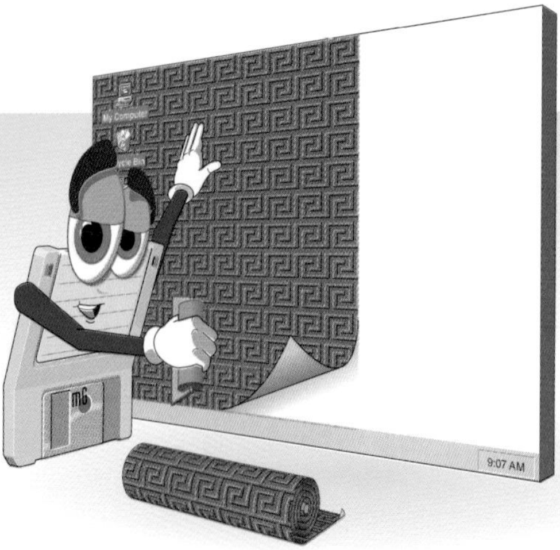

ADD WALLPAPER

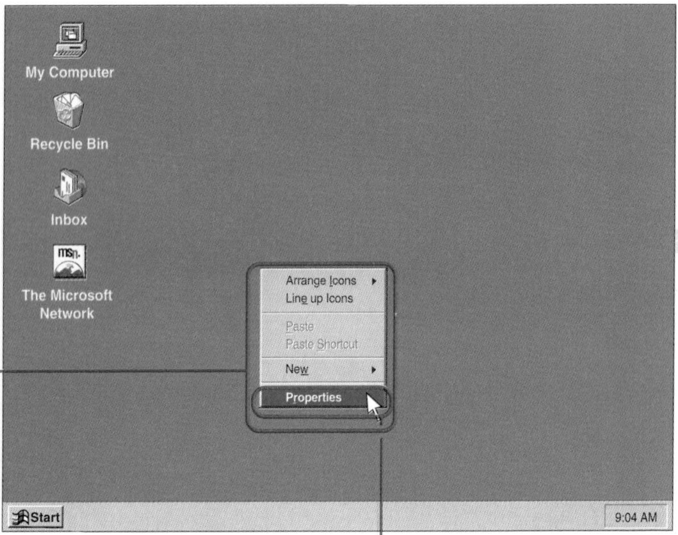

1 Move the mouse over a blank area on your screen and then press the **right** button. A menu appears.

2 Move the mouse over **Properties** and then press the left button.

◆ The **Display Properties** dialog box appears.

You can decorate your screen by adding wallpaper.

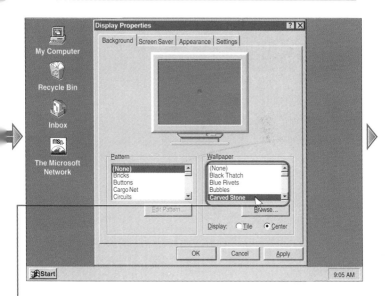

3 Move the mouse ⌖ over the wallpaper you want to display (example: **Carved Stone**) and then press the left button.

Note: To view all the available wallpapers, use the scroll bar. For more information, refer to page 50.

171

ADD WALLPAPER

These are some of the wallpapers Windows offers.

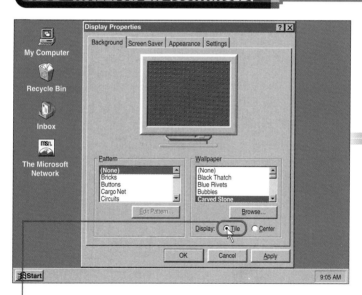

4 To cover your entire screen with the wallpaper you selected, move the mouse ⃠ over **Tile** and then press the left button (○ changes to ◉).

*Note: To place a small wallpaper image in the middle of your screen, select the **Center** option.*

172

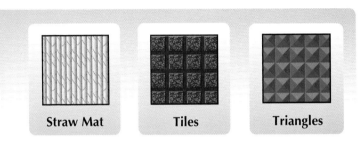

Straw Mat   **Tiles**   **Triangles**

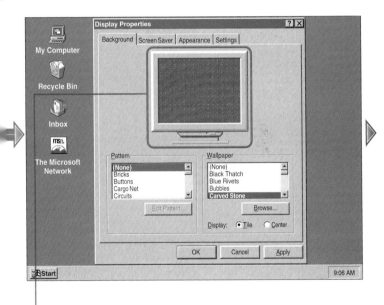

◆ This area displays
how the wallpaper you
selected will look on
your screen.

ADD WALLPAPER

ADD WALLPAPER (CONTINUED)

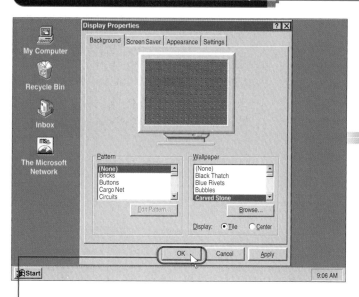

5 To display the wallpaper on
your screen, move the mouse ⌖
over **OK** and then press the left button.

174

Adding
wallpaper enhances
the appearance of
your screen.

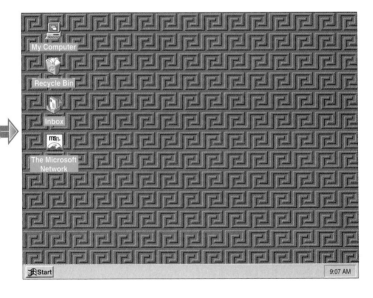

◆ Your screen displays
the wallpaper you
selected.

Note: To remove wallpaper from your
screen, perform steps **1** to **3**
starting on page 170, selecting **(None)**
in step **3**. Then perform step **5**.

175

CHANGE SCREEN COLORS

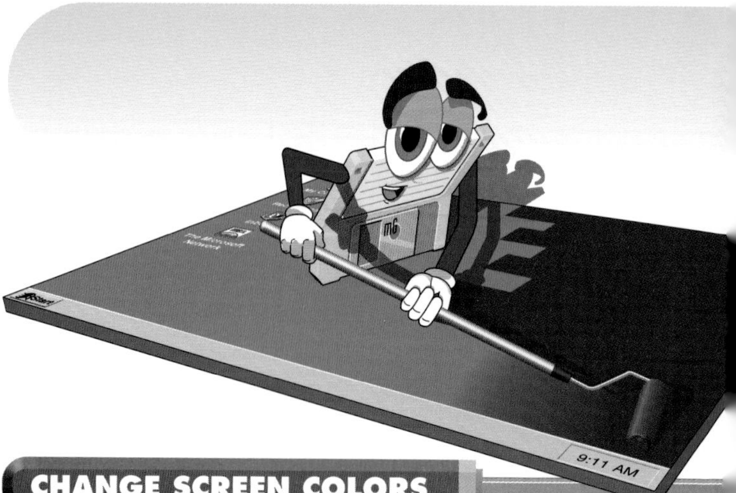

CHANGE SCREEN COLORS

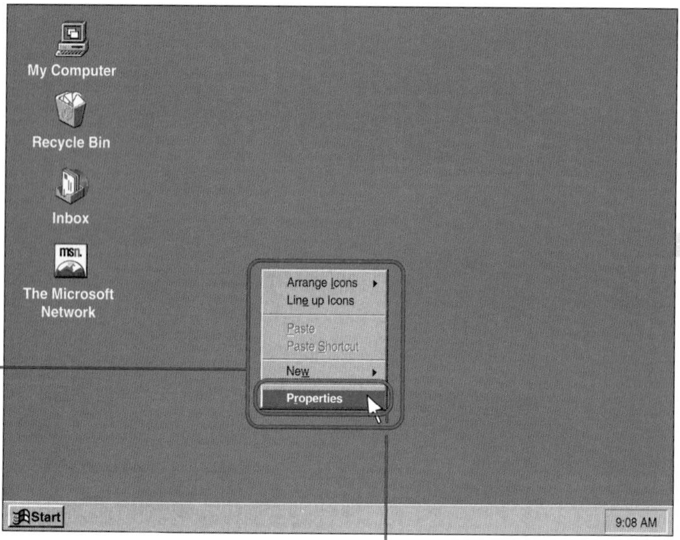

1 Move the mouse over a blank area on your screen and then press the **right** button. A menu appears.

2 Move the mouse over **Properties** and then press the left button.

You can change the colors displayed on your screen to suit your preferences.

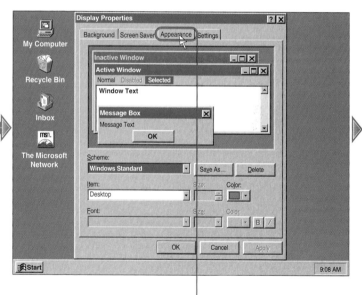

◆ The **Display Properties** dialog box appears.

3 Move the mouse ⍺ over the **Appearance** tab and then press the left button.

CONTINUED

177

CHANGE SCREEN COLORS

These are some of the color schemes Windows offers.

CHANGE SCREEN COLORS (CONTINUED)

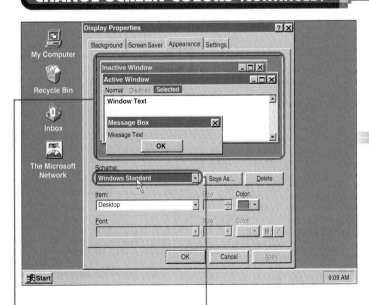

◆ This area displays the current color scheme.

4 To display a list of the available color schemes, move the mouse ▷ over this area and then press the left button.

178

Wheat

Rose

Teal (VGA)

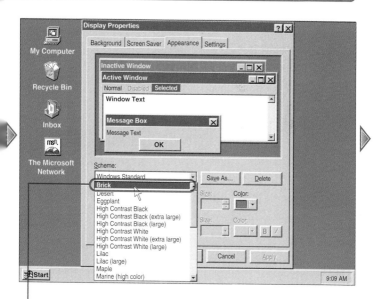

5 Move the mouse ⬉ over the color scheme you want to use (example: **Brick**) and then press the left button.

Note: To view all the available color schemes, use the scroll bar. For more information, refer to page 50.

CONTINUED

(179)

CHANGE SCREEN COLORS

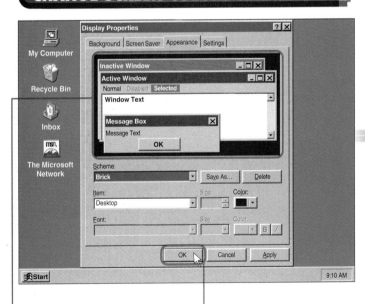

◆ This area displays how your screen will look with the color scheme you selected.

6 To apply the color scheme, move the mouse over **OK** and then press the left button.

180

Changing your screen colors enhances the appearance of your screen.

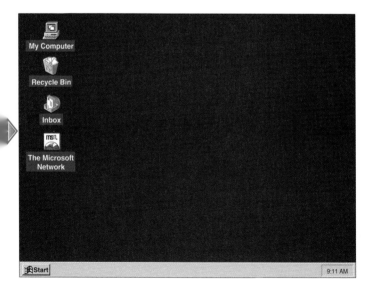

◆ Your screen displays the color scheme you selected.

Note: To return to the original color scheme, repeat steps 1 to 6 starting on page 176, selecting Windows Standard in step 5.

SET UP A SCREEN SAVER

SET UP A SCREEN SAVER

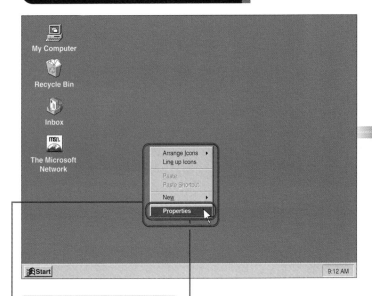

My Computer

Recycle Bin

Inbox

The Microsoft Network

Arrange Icons ▶
Line up Icons

Paste
Paste Shortcut

New ▶

Properties

Start   9:12 AM

1 Move the mouse ⟍ over a blank area on your screen and then press the **right** button. A menu appears.

2 Move the mouse ⟍ over **Properties** and then press the left button.

A screen saver is a moving picture or pattern that appears on the screen when you do not use your computer for a period of time.

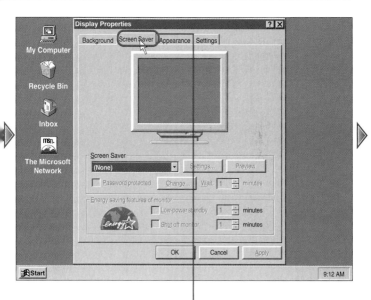

◆ The **Display Properties** dialog box appears.

3 Move the mouse ↘ over the **Screen Saver** tab and then press the left button.

CONTINUED

183

SET UP A SCREEN SAVER

Screen savers were originally designed to prevent screen burn, which occurs when an image appears in a fixed position for a period of time.

SET UP A SCREEN SAVER (CONTINUED)

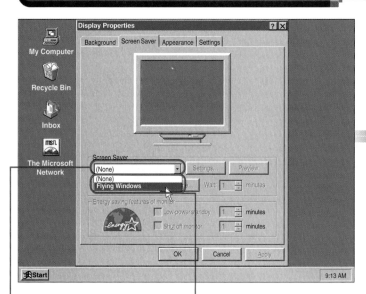

4 Move the mouse ⤢ over this area and then press the left button.

5 Move the mouse ⤢ over **Flying Windows** and then press the left button.

Note: You can buy sophisticated screen savers at most computer stores.

Today's monitors are better designed to prevent screen burn, but people still use screen savers for entertainment.

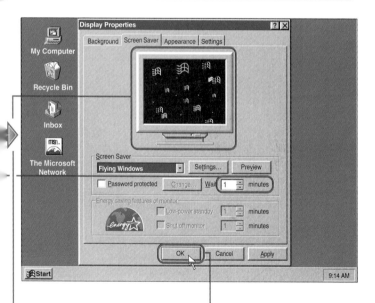

◆ This area displays how the screen saver will look on your screen.

→ The screen saver will appear when you do not use your computer for the amount of time displayed in this area.

6 Move the mouse ⬚ over **OK** and then press the left button.

CHANGE MOUSE SETTINGS

CHANGE MOUSE SETTINGS

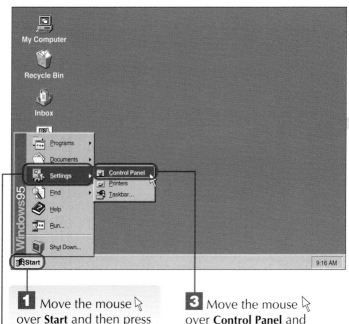

1 Move the mouse ▷ over **Start** and then press the left button.

2 Move the mouse ▷ over **Settings**.

3 Move the mouse ▷ over **Control Panel** and then press the left button.

You can change the way your mouse works to suit your needs.

♦ The **Control Panel** window appears.

4 To change the mouse settings, move the mouse over **Mouse** and then quickly press the left button twice.

♦ The **Mouse Properties** dialog box appears.

CONTINUED

187

CHANGE MOUSE SETTINGS

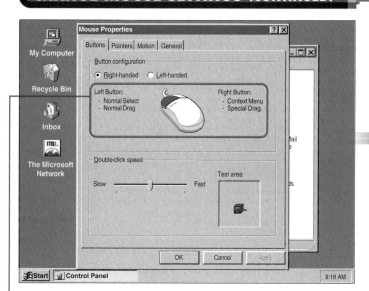

SWITCH BUTTONS

◆ This area describes the current functions of the left and right mouse buttons.

188

If you are left-handed, you can switch the functions of the left and right mouse buttons to make the mouse easier to use.

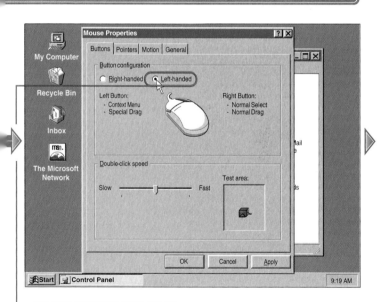

1 To switch the functions of the buttons, move the mouse ⌖ over this option and then press the left button (○ changes to ⊙).

Note: This change will not take effect until you confirm the changes. To do so, refer to page 193.

CONTINUED

189

CHANGE MOUSE SETTINGS

CHANGE MOUSE SETTINGS (CONTINUED)

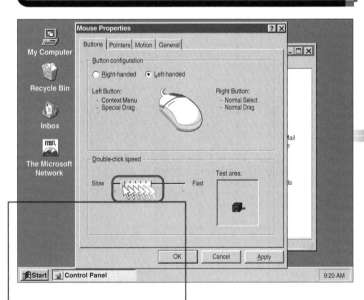

DOUBLE-CLICK SPEED

1 To change the double-click speed, move the mouse ⌖ over ⟧.

2 Press and hold down the left button as you drag ⟧ to increase or decrease the double-click speed. Then release the button.

Note: If you are an inexperienced mouse user, you may find a slower speed easier to use.

You can change
the amount of time that
can pass between two clicks
of the mouse button for
Windows to recognize a
double-click.

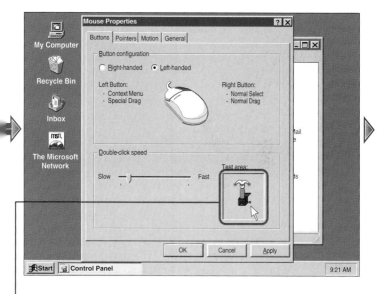

3 To test the double-click speed, move the mouse � over this area and then quickly press the left button twice.

◆ The jack-in-the-box appears if you clicked at the correct speed.

Note: This change will not take effect until you confirm the changes. To do so, refer to page 193.

CONTINUED

191

CHANGE MOUSE SETTINGS

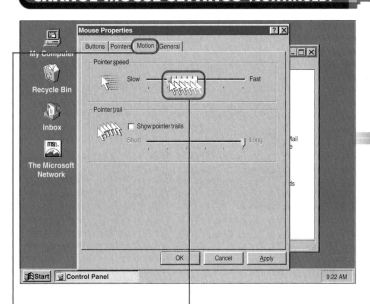

POINTER SPEED

1 Move the mouse ⊾ over the **Motion** tab and then press the left button.

2 To change the pointer speed, move the mouse ⊾ over ⬛.

3 Press and hold down the left button as you drag ⬛ to increase or decrease the pointer speed. Then release the button.

192

You can make
the mouse pointer
on your screen move
faster or slower.

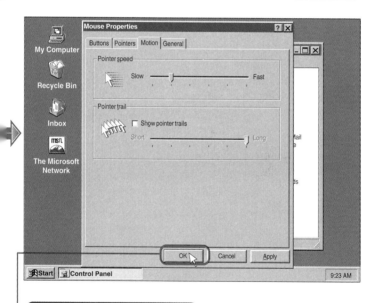

CONFIRM CHANGES

1 When you finish
selecting all the mouse
settings you want to change,
move the mouse ⬡ over **OK**
and then press the left button.

MAINTAIN YOUR COMPUTER

Format a Disk

Detect and Repair Disk Errors

Defragment a Disk

MicroFLOPPY
Double Sided
720 Kb

MicroFLOPPY
Double Sided
1.44 Mb

FORMAT A DISK

Formatting Disks

Track

Sector

FORMAT A DISK

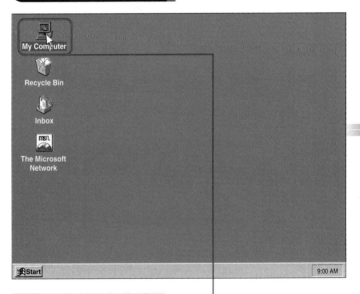

My Computer

Recycle Bin

Inbox

The Microsoft
Network

Start

9:00 AM

1 Insert the floppy disk you want to format into a drive.

2 Move the mouse over **My Computer** and then quickly press the left button twice.

You must format a floppy disk before you can use it to store information.

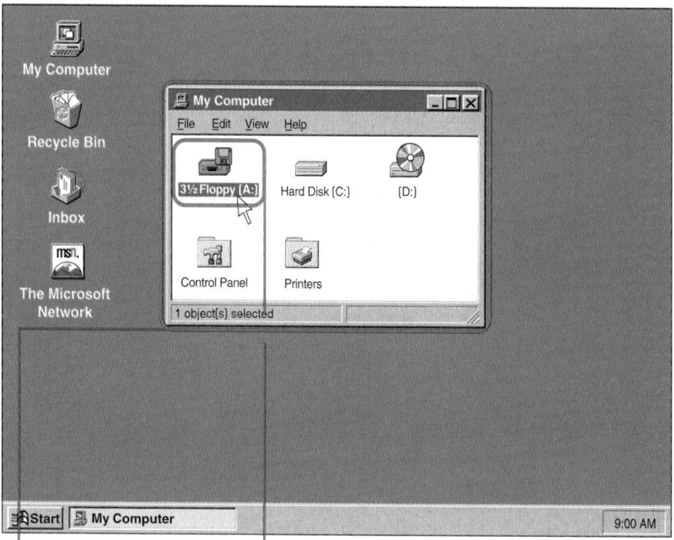

◆ The **My Computer** window appears.

3 Move the mouse ⇖ over the drive containing the floppy disk you want to format (example: **A:**) and then press the left button.

CONTINUED

FORMAT A DISK

FORMAT A DISK (CONTINUED)

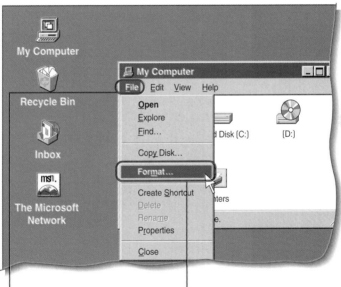

My Computer

Recycle Bin

Inbox

msn.
The Microsoft
Network

My Computer

File   Edit   View   Help

Open
Explore
Find...

Copy Disk...

Format...

Create Shortcut
Delete
Rename
Properties

Close

d Disk [C:]   [D:]

nters

e.

4 Move the mouse ⌖
over **File** and then press
the left button.

5 Move the mouse ⌖
over **Format** and then
press the left button.

◆ The **Format** dialog
box appears.

Before formatting a floppy disk, make sure the disk does not contain information you want to keep. Formatting will remove all the information on the disk.

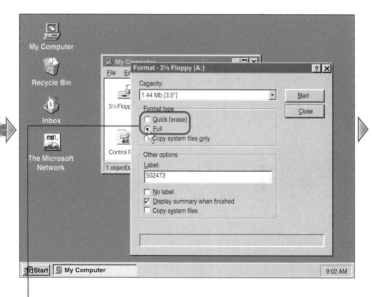

6 Move the mouse ⌖ over the type of format you want to perform and then press the left button (○ changes to ⦿). If the floppy disk has never been formatted, select the **Full** option.

Quick (erase)

Removes all files but does not scan the disk for damaged areas.

Full

Removes all files and scans the disk for damaged areas.

CONTINUED

FORMAT A DISK

When formatting a floppy disk, you must tell Windows how much information the disk can hold.

HIGH-DENSITY 1.44 Mb

A 3.5 inch floppy disk that has two holes and displays the HD symbol holds 1.44 Mb of information.

MicroFLOPPY
Double Sided
1.44 Mb

FORMAT A DISK (CONTINUED)

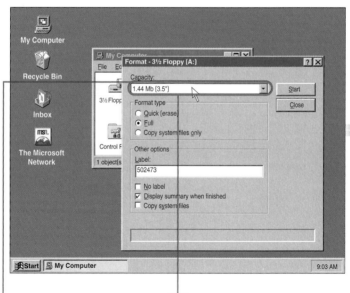

My Computer

Recycle Bin

Inbox

The Microsoft Network

Format - 3½ Floppy (A:)

Capacity:
1.44 Mb (3.5")

Format type
- Quick (erase)
- Full
- Copy system files only

Other options
Label:
502473

- No label
- Display summary when finished
- Copy system files

Start
Close

Start | My Computer   9:03 AM

◆ This area displays how much information the floppy disk can hold.

7 To select a different capacity, move the mouse over this area and then press the left button.

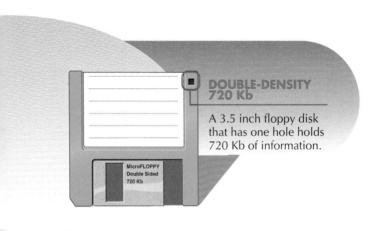

DOUBLE-DENSITY 720 Kb

A 3.5 inch floppy disk that has one hole holds 720 Kb of information.

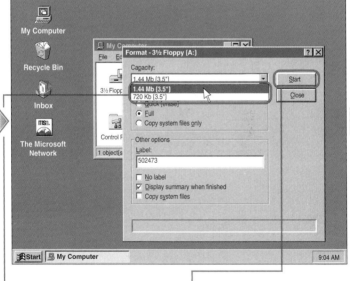

8 Move the mouse Ⓚ over the capacity you want and then press the left button.

9 To start formatting the floppy disk, move the mouse Ⓚ over **Start** and then press the left button.

CONTINUED

201

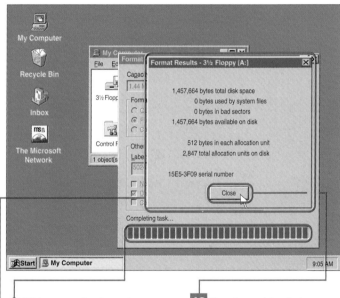

◆ This area displays the progress of the format.

◆ The **Format Results** dialog box appears when the format is complete. It displays information about the formatted disk.

10 To close this dialog box, move the mouse over **Close** and then press the left button.

When the format is complete, you can use the disk to store information.

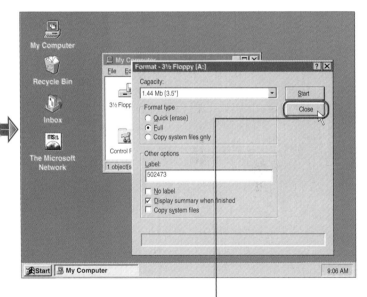

◆ To format another floppy disk, insert the disk and then repeat steps **6** to **10** starting on page 199.

11 To close the **Format** dialog box, move the mouse ᗄ over **Close** and then press the left button.

DETECT AND REPAIR DISK ERRORS

Hard Disk

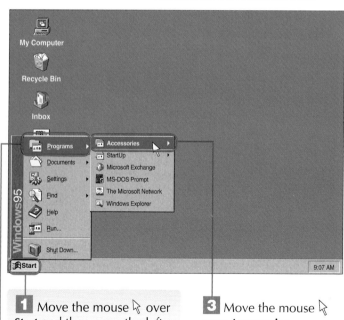

1 Move the mouse ↖ over **Start** and then press the left button.

2 Move the mouse ↖ over **Programs**.

3 Move the mouse ↖ over **Accessories**.

204

You can improve the performance of your computer by using ScanDisk to search for and repair disk errors.

The hard disk is the primary device that a computer uses to store information.

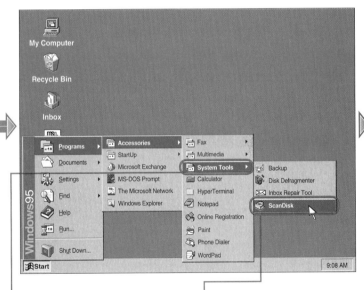

4 Move the mouse ⋄ over **System Tools**.

5 Move the mouse ⋄ over **ScanDisk** and then press the left button.

CONTINUED

205

DETECT AND REPAIR DISK ERRORS

DETECT AND REPAIR (CONTINUED)

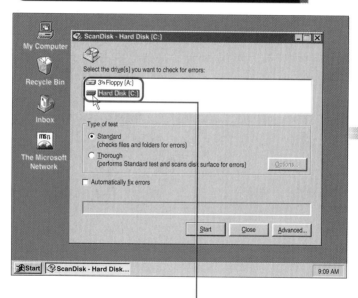

◆ The **ScanDisk** dialog box appears.

6 Move the mouse ⃗ over the drive you want to check for errors (example: **C:**) and then press the left button.

You must specify what type of test you want ScanDisk to perform.

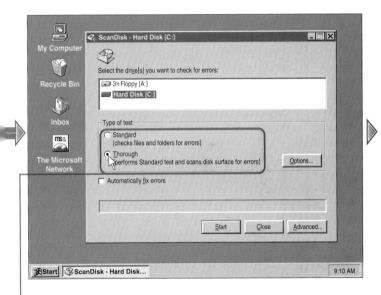

7 Move the mouse ⤶ over the type of test you want to perform (example: **Thorough**) and then press the left button. ○ changes to ⦿.

Standard
Checks files and folders for errors.
Thorough
Checks files, folders and the disk surface for errors.

CONTINUED

207

DETECT AND REPAIR DISK ERRORS

DETECT AND REPAIR (CONTINUED)

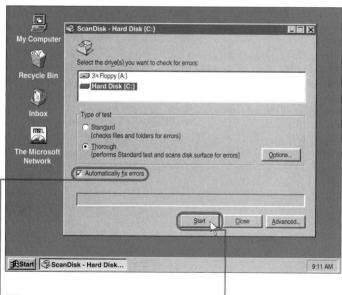

8 If you want Windows to automatically repair any disk errors it finds, move the mouse ⤢ over this option and then press the left button (☐ changes to ☑).

9 To start the check, move the mouse ⤢ over **Start** and then press the left button.

You can have Windows automatically repair any disk errors it finds.

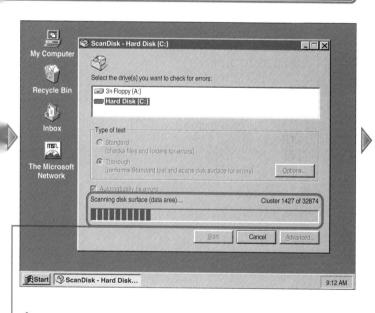

◆ This area displays the progress of the check.

DETECT AND REPAIR DISK ERRORS

DETECT AND REPAIR (CONTINUED)

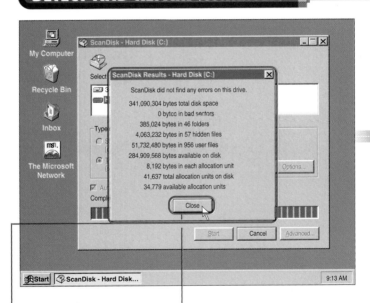

◆ The **ScanDisk Results** dialog box appears when the check is complete. It displays information about the disk.

10 To close this dialog box, move the mouse ⬚ over **Close** and then press the left button.

You should check your hard disk for errors at least once a month.

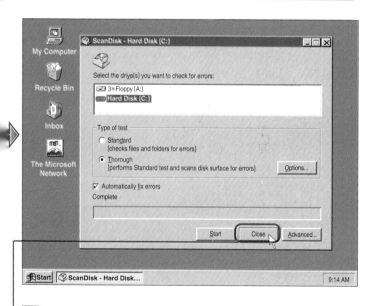

11 To close the **ScanDisk** dialog box, move the mouse ⫯ over **Close** and then press the left button.

DEFRAGMENT A DISK

DEFRAGMENT A DISK

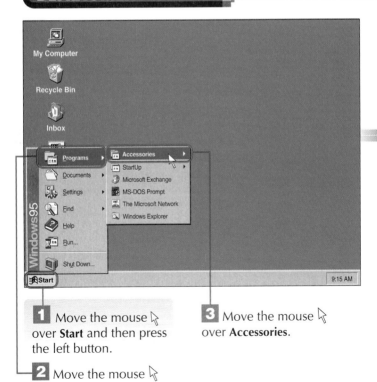

1 Move the mouse ⌖ over **Start** and then press the left button.

2 Move the mouse ⌖ over **Programs**.

3 Move the mouse ⌖ over **Accessories**.

212

You can improve the performance of your computer by using the Disk Defragmenter program.

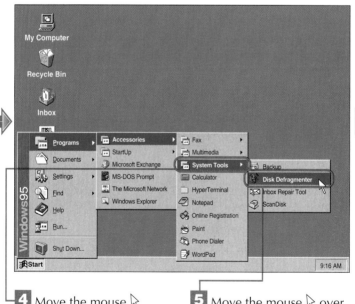

4 Move the mouse ⟍ over **System Tools**.

5 Move the mouse ⟍ over **Disk Defragmenter** and then press the left button.

CONTINUED

213

DEFRAGMENT A DISK

DEFRAGMENT A DISK (CONTINUED)

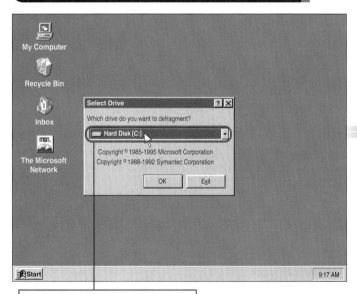

◆ This area displays the drive that Windows will defragment.

6 To select a different drive, move the mouse ⌐ over this area and then press the left button.

The Disk Defragmenter program reorganizes the files stored on your hard disk. This reduces the time the computer will spend locating a file.

◆ A list of the drives on your computer appears.

CONTINUED

7 Move the mouse ⟍ over the drive you want to defragment (example: **C:**) and then press the left button.

215

DEFRAGMENT A DISK

PRINTING...

DEFRAGMENT A DISK (CONTINUED)

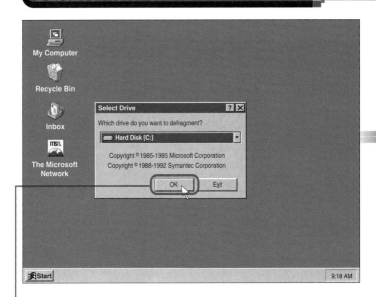

8 Move the mouse ⌖ over **OK** and then press the left button.

You can perform other tasks on your computer while Windows defragments a disk, but your computer will operate slower.

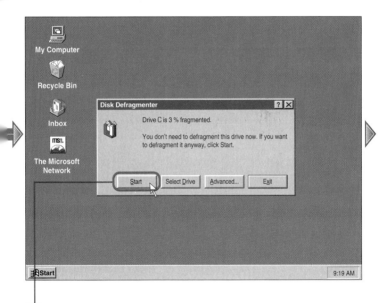

9 Move the mouse ⬚ over **Start** and then press the left button.

CONTINUED

217

DEFRAGMENT A DISK

DEFRAGMENT A DISK (CONTINUED)

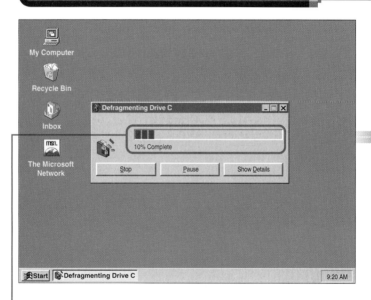

◆ This area displays
the progress of the
defragmentation.

You should defragment your hard disk at least once a month.

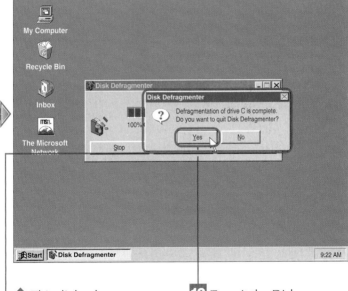

◆ This dialog box appears when the defragmentation is complete.

10 To exit the Disk Defragmenter program, move the mouse ▷ over **Yes** and then press the left button.

INDEX

INDEX

ORDER FORM

Qty	ISBN	Title	Price	Total

Shipping & Handling Charges

	Description	Each First book	add'l. book	Total
Domestic	Normal	$4.50	$1.50	$
	Two Day Air	$8.50	$2.50	$
	Overnight	$18.00	$3.00	$
International	Surface	$8.00	$8.00	$
	Airmail	$16.00	$16.00	$
	DHL Air	$17.00	$17.00	$

Subtotal _____

CA residents add
applicable sales tax _____

IN, MA and MD
residents add
5% sales tax _____

IL, residents add
6.25% sales tax _____

RI residents add
7% sales tax _____

TX residents add
8.25% sales tax _____

Shipping _____

Total _____

Ship to:

Name _____

Address _____

Company _____

City/State/Zip _____

Daytime Phone _____

Payment: □ Check to IDG Books (US Funds Only)

□ Visa   □ Mastercard   □ American Express

Card # _____ Exp. _____

Signature _____

IDG Books Education Group
Jim Kelly, Director of Education Sales – 9 Village Circle, Ste. 450, Westlake, TX 76262
800-434-2086 Phone • 817-430-5852 Fax • 8:30-5:00 CST

SUPER STAR

Macs For Dummies,™
2nd Edition
by David Pogue

ISBN: 1-56884-051-9
$19.95 USA/$26.95 Canada

Over
12 Million
in print!

The Internet
For Dummies™
by John Levine &
Carol Baroudi!

ISBN: 1-56884-024-1
$19.95 USA/$26.95 Canada

SUPER STAR

DOS For Dummies,®
2nd Edition
by Dan Gookin

ISBN: 1-878058-75-4
$16.95 USA/$22.95 Canada